The Field Guide to

SPORTS METAPHORS

The Field Guide to
SPORTS METAPHORS

A Compendium of
Competitive Words and Idioms

JOSH CHETWYND

TEN SPEED PRESS
Berkeley

Copyright © 2016 by Josh Chetwynd

Published in the United States by Ten Speed Press,
an imprint of the Crown Publishing Group, a division
of Penguin Random House LLC, New York.
www.crownpublishing.com
www.tenspeed.com

Ten Speed Press and the Ten Speed Press colophon are
registered trademarks of Penguin Random House LLC.

Library of Congress Cataloging-in-Publication Data
Chetwynd, Josh, 1971-
Field guide to sports metaphors : a compendium of
competitive words and idioms / Josh Chetwynd.
First Edition. | New York : Ten Speed Press, [2016] | Includes
  bibliographical references and index.
LCSH: English language—Terms and phrases. | English
  language—Figures of speech. | English language—Idioms—
Dictionaries. | Sports—Terminology.
LCC PE1689 .C53 2016 | DDC 808/.032—dc23
LC record available at http://lccn.loc.gov/2015031726

Hardcover ISBN: 978-1-60774-811-3
eBook ISBN: 978-1-60774-812-0

Printed in the United States of America

Design by Nami Kurita

10 9 8 7 6 5 4 3 2 1

First Edition

For my parents, Gloria and Lionel,
and my brother Michael

CONTENTS

Introduction
1

Part I. Team Sports

1. BASEBALL
7

2. BASKETBALL
43

3. FOOTBALL
55

4. HOCKEY
73

5. SOCCER
81

Part II. Individual Sports

6. AUTO RACING
89

7. BILLIARDS (POOL)
95

8. BOWLING
103

9. BOXING
107

10. GOLF
129

11. HORSE RACING
137

12. TENNIS
163

13. TRACK AND FIELD (RUNNING)
169

14. WRESTLING
179

Free Agents: Unattached
Sports Idioms and Words
188

Endnotes
200

Further Reading
209

Acknowledgments
210

About the Author
212

Index of Idioms and Words
213

INTRODUCTION

English has relied on many performance enhancers to build its immensely rich vocabulary.* Sure, Shakespeare and the Bible have led the way, but this book is a reminder that sports have also played a huge role in bulking up our language. Quite simply, the games we love and the athletic endeavors we play have been essential when it comes to developing our everyday phrases and words.

How pervasive is this gift? Look no further than the long line of presidents who have leaned on sports for linguistic assistance. For example, when Teddy Roosevelt decided he'd run for president in 1912, he relied on boxing chatter, saying, "My hat is in the ring."**

Richard Nixon's affinity for sports idioms was well known. Many believe he popularized the expression *game plan* outside of its football beginnings. He was also a fan of applying the *full-court press* even when there wasn't a basketball in sight. (Search Wikipedia under the heading "Watergate," if you want additional details.)

This political attraction hasn't diminished over the years. In 2014, Barack Obama went thoroughly sporty when discussing his approach to foreign policy. "You hit singles, you hit doubles; every once in a while we may be able to hit a home run," he told NPR in an interview he peppered with a score of other sports analogies.

---

* Estimates of the size of the English lexicon range from at least 250,000 to more than a million words, depending on the source of the data and how you define a word (e.g., Does slang count? Should scientific terms be included?).

** For citations for all quotations in this book, please turn to the endnotes section beginning on page 200.

There's a reason why our leaders (and everybody else from lawyers to layabouts) are drawn to this type of speech. As the longtime *New York Times* language columnist William Safire once wrote, politicians seek out sports metaphors because they "relate closely to many people." Indeed, the evocative words we hear on the grass and dirt of local ball fields or around the sweat-stained canvases of boxing rings resonate because they are familiar.

Of course, it's not just hearing them regularly that makes them popular. (Every man is told to "turn your head and cough" each time he goes to the doctor's office for a hernia exam, but nobody uses that as a figure of speech.) No, it's the competitive, and often inspirational, nature of sports that's a difference maker. Even in the best of times we're vying for something—money, love, a good parking spot. So it makes sense that when we dig deep for words to express our personal turmoil or we want to revel in our success, we mine the world of ritualized contests for the right sentiments.

Now there are some naysayers who believe this longstanding trend isn't a good thing. In 1976, writer Francine Hardaway penned an article for a journal called *College English* titled "Foul Play: Sports Metaphors as Public Doublespeak." She feared that sports idioms had become "language meant to manipulate its audience unconsciously."

But in defense of the sports words we wield, which imagery-invoking phrases or metaphors aren't trying to sway listeners for better or for worse? As George Orwell said generally about euphemisms (language used to soften the real meaning of something): They are designed "to make lies sound truthful and murder respectable."

On a less depressing—yet equally critical—note, some take issue with how clichéd sports idioms and words have become.

In 2014, the satirical doyens at *The Onion* ran a faux letter from a father to a son. The piece lampooned: "Son, I think it's high time you and I sat down and touched base. As your father, it's been difficult watching you drop the ball these past few months. . . . Your head just hasn't been in the game, and sadly for me, I've had a ringside seat as you've repeatedly struck out."

It's true that some turns of phrase have become vastly overused. Popularity has its downside. But whether you like it or not, this type of talk tends to be sticky. Nearly any conversation will include some language from this book. Appreciating a little of the history behind these expressions gives you a conversational advantage over the average metaphor-toting colleague. It means you'll be the one deftly freshening up even the most trite sports idiom by dropping a bit of additional knowledge.

All that said, we shouldn't be so hard on this avenue of speech. While we may roll our eyes when a colleague says he'll *pinch-hit* at a meeting, not everything in this space is thoroughly worn out. Terms like *fluke*, *bias,* and *jazz* have all brightened our language thanks to sports—and are all discussed in this volume.

With that in mind, the purpose of this book is to offer a robust—and fun—survey of the origins and histories of the words and idioms we've taken from athletic competitions and applied to our ordinary and often sedentary lives (along with those seemingly sports-inspired terms that actually lack on-the-field beginnings . . . for instance, *keep the ball rolling*).

But before we get there, a quick language explanation: an idiomatic phrase is a series of words used to signify something other than their obvious meaning. So, idiomatically speaking, when a business opportunity is a *slam dunk*, we're not talking about stuffing a ball down a hoop. Instead, it means it's a sure thing.

As a result, this book doesn't look at memorable sports phrases that haven't crossed over into regular conversation. So as much as I like bowling's *seven-ten split*, until people start using it generically to explain a difficult situation ("Man, I'm late on that assignment; I'm sure facing a seven-ten split"), it doesn't make the cut.

I must also note there are some activities, like swimming, sailing, and archery, that are most certainly practiced in sports, but don't show up here. The reason: So many of the expressions that have developed in these endeavors aren't from the formal sporting elements of the pursuit. For instance, *dipping your toe in the water* definitely may happen before competing in the one hundred–meter butterfly, but the phrase comes from the recreational aspects of swimming rather than the sport. (Similarly, nautical idioms almost invariably started with the travel or trading aspects of shipping, not yachting competitions.)

Beyond that, while this book aims to be comprehensive, it's not exhaustive. If you don't find a phrase or word you were sure should have been included, I suggest one of three things. First, it may be here but just not where you'd expect it (peruse the index before, ahem, *jumping the gun* with frustration). Second, the expression you assumed came from sports may actually have originated or been popularized elsewhere. (I've tried to note lots of these sayings, but it's hard to catch all of them.) Finally, I could have just *struck out* (which, by the way, you can find on page 38). If it's the latter, apologies. Nevertheless, I hope I've made up for it with a multitude of other interesting tales.

Part I

TEAM SPORTS

Chapter 1

BASEBALL

**"I'd say that's in the ballpark ...
but a ballpark that needed renovation."**

—Producer Dick Wolf on reports that it would cost
$550 million to keep *Law and Order* going in 2003

BALLPARK FIGURE

In the early years of the Vietnam conflict, the U.S. Army and Air Force repurposed the phrase *ballpark figure* to sidestep questions about personnel and weapons. As one journalist put it in 1968, each military ballpark figure was purely a "guesstimate."

That officers opted for baseball tabulations, which are some of the most exacting numbers (think slugging percentages or earned run averages), was an interesting choice. But maybe PR folks at the Pentagon thought pulling in America's national pastime softened the blow of being vague (baseball, apple pie, and the fog of war, perhaps?).

In defense of the armed forces, the phrase was likely first manipulated by members of a very young NASA at the end of the 1950s. Yes, you can probably blame rocket scientists for the seeming inconsistency. With so much unclear at the dawn of the space age (like identifying satellite capsule recovery areas), spitballing was sometimes necessary.

By the beginning of the 1970s, publications were comfortable enough with the concept to cease putting quotes around *ballpark* and deployed the expression for all sorts of purposes (although local government spending seemed to be a popular subject for this type of estimating).

Ballpark figure has a sister idiom, *in the ballpark*, which is sort of like when your ballpark figure is generally correct. Both became trendy around the same time. Veteran *New York Times* word columnist William Safire explained why stadiums had metaphorical appeal during baseball's 1960s heyday: "The ballpark was used as a microcosm: To be 'in the ballpark' (even if out in left field) was to be 'in this world.'"

BATTING A THOUSAND

You may be thinking of baseball when you gush about your buddy *batting a thousand* after concocting two or three excellent batches of margaritas, but the reality is that such an achievement—however epic—is nearly antithetical to the sport. The reason: In a game where earning a base hit just 30 percent of the time usually confers all-star status, the idea of being "perfect" at the plate isn't really an achievable goal.

Ponder the fact that more than eighteen thousand people have competed at the Major League Baseball level. Of that group, only eighty-four own flawless 1.000 career batting averages, according to Jeff Zimmerman at FanGraphs, a company that specializes in baseball statistics. That's less than 0.5 percent of all baseball players. And those with spotless records can attribute their achievement in large part to limited opportunities: the guy who was able to do it with the most plate appearances—John Paciorek—had only three official at bats. (In fact, his career was less than perfect as he appeared in only one big-league contest for the Houston Colt 45s in 1963 before severe back problems cut his playing days short.)

Despite that reality, *batting a thousand* entered print by 1911. At first, it was primarily used as a turn of phrase in stories about baseball and other sports. For example, a 1927 article on New York Yankees great Babe Ruth gushed that the slugger was "batting a thousand for popularity honors." The Babe himself was also a fan of the metaphor, using it at a Salvation Army fundraising event earlier in the decade. "A home run . . . means at least a dollar from you and a dollar from me," he said in 1921. "Let's bat a thousand percent."

Over time the saying has been used to laud nearly everything. The list of people, groups, and things supposedly batting a thousand has included the Alton, Illinois, City Court; weather in Racine, Wisconsin; safe-cracking robbers in Montana; a referee at a wrestling match in Greeley, Colorado; and Robert Redford. That said, like a baseball player who has one great day, none of them probably maintained their pristine record (sorry, Mr. Redford).

BIG LEAGUES

Making the *big leagues* of your profession—whether you're an accountant or a baseball player—is a lot like entering the Emerald City in *The Wizard of Oz*. It's immediately clear you've stepped up in class. Still, in most walks of life, defining just what the big leagues are isn't an exact science. There's no absolute list of big-league veterinarians or fire stations. It's typically one of those you-know-it-when-you-see-it things.

From a sporting standpoint, it's more precise—though it took some time to get there. While, nowadays, we reflexively recognize Major League Baseball as synonymous with the big leagues, in the beginning, there was just a singular big league. The National League, founded in 1876, enjoyed a brief period as the one-stop locale for making it to the pinnacle of professional baseball.

But the concept went plural pretty quickly with additional circuits receiving the exalted status—depending on whom you listened to. In 1890, for example, many newspapers included box scores for a renegade organization called the Players' League under the headline "The Big Leagues." The American Association, which ran from 1882 to 1891, was another outlet judged part of the big leagues. Even in the modern era, some baseball historians have argued over whether the Federal League (1914–1915) deserved big-league cred.

As even casual fans can tell you, the ultimate winners of this competition were the aforementioned National League along with the American League, which fully took root in 1901. That said, they didn't formally brand themselves Major League Baseball until the 1960s, and the two circuits didn't actually merge until 2000.

Even with all this initial uncertainty, early twentieth-century writers loved the phrase, expanding the scope of its meaning and usage. One *New York Tribune* journalist twisted it a bit in 1917 when talking about his state's Tammany Hall political machine, and its need to put forward a "big-league candidate." Another more current variation is *big-leaguing* for when a person acts in an arrogant manner (as in "That B-level celebrity just big-leagued me by taking my table at the restaurant").

BUSH LEAGUES

Being in the *bush leagues* is akin to being in the backwoods. According to one theory, the expression takes its cue from the Dutch word *bosch*, which means wilderness, and led to the English term *bush*. So if you're in the bush leagues, you're far from civilization, and if you're a *bush leaguer*, well, you might as well be living with wolves. From a baseball perspective, the term could have also been created to contrast the poorly kept bushy fields in small towns and the Major Leagues' pristine diamonds.

Whatever the inspiration, there appears to be one early circuit that was the first to embrace the phrase. The Iowa-South Dakota League, which competed in 1902 and 1903, literally called itself "the Bush League." Did that circuit spawn the expression? Well, we do know that the term was applied regularly to recognize any low-level minor league just after that circuit was founded and carried on into nonbaseball usage by the next decade.

While bush league teams may be in the wild, it hasn't stopped many of them from having fun with their obscurity. Some off-center bush league club nicknames have included the Oswego (New York) Starchboxes, the Eau Claire (Wisconsin) Cream Puffs, the Borger (Texas) Gassers, the Kirksville (Missouri) Osteopaths, and the Zanesville (Ohio) Flood Sufferers.

Of course, the disparity between the bush leagues and the big leagues presumably led to another class-based idiom: *out of your league*. And, to be fair, when you're playing with the Flood Sufferers instead of the Los Angeles Dodgers, it's hard to argue otherwise.

COVER ALL THE BASES

Imagine, instead of *covering all the bases* or *covering your bases* during an important conference call, you said *soaking all the runners* or *patching your runners*. Equally as bewildering, what if rather than *touching base* with someone, you described that brief chat as *making post*? As odd as it sounds, it could have happened.

Let's rewind to the primeval days of baseball: In the beginning, bases as we know them weren't required. Instead of those softish, white fifteen-inch squares, wooden posts were often stuck into the ground (like those used in a British predecessor to baseball called rounders). As a result, players weren't required to "touch" anything, but simply "make" it (i.e., get to the location). In other words, a player wouldn't touch base but would actually make post. Ultimately, baseball potentates didn't care for either the sticks or the "making" bit. So the requirement for square canvas bases—filled with sand or sawdust—was written into the rules in 1857, and the necessity to make physical contact became baseball law six years later.

As for *covering bases*, it wasn't as important a strategic point in early baseball. You see, players on defense could originally pelt an opposing runner with the ball to get him out, effectively cutting the base (and fellow fielders) from the equation. In gentlemen's terms, this was known as *soaking* or *patching*. Evidently, black-and-blue players quickly realized this wasn't very civil, and the act was prohibited in 1845 (though crusty New Englanders apparently continued the practice into the 1860s). Mercifully, we don't have to soak all the runners nowadays; we can just try to cover all the bases.

Despite the relatively early modifications to these rules, the phrases that benefited from this evolution didn't develop until much later. The *Oxford English Dictionary* has *touch base* first entering print in 1918, but, for the most part, none of these variants was a fixture in common speech until the 1950s.

CURVEBALL

Though he had a name that was more Willy Wonka than ace pitcher, W. Arthur "Candy" Cummings earned a place in baseball's Hall of Fame thanks to one special creation. No, it wasn't a Gobstopper; it was the *curveball*. Growing up in Brooklyn in the mid-nineteenth century, Cummings became an expert at flinging clam shells with astonishing movement at his local beach. In a eureka moment, he fathomed that if he twirled a baseball similarly it would also swerve.

After four years of trial and error, the eighteen-year-old right-hander mastered his signature pitch in 1867. In what must have been seen as a dark art by many opposing hitters,

Cummings's curveball was so unhittable that in 1871, he was named the sport's outstanding player by the game's top writer at the time, Henry Chadwick. The pitch's unexpected movement was also the impetus for commonly using the word to explain a surprising twist.

But here's the curveball on the curveball: at one point, gadflies and even some scientists believed the pitch didn't truly move and, instead, was an optical illusion. This argument played out in the pages of an unexpectedly wide array of periodicals, including the *New Yorker*, *Life,* and the *American Journal of Physics*. Early tests supported the claim that the ball didn't really change course.

A brief game changer: Cricket

English wouldn't be the same without the language of the British pastime cricket. Just check out "Hat trick" (see page 76) for back up. Here are a few other terms used in the sport that have idiomatically crossed the Atlantic (along with a good one that hasn't):

A hit. Though the word predates cricket, the sport made it tremendously popular. It was definitely pilfered by baseball and, perhaps, by the theater (and elsewhere), where it's used to describe a big success.

Had a good innings. While Americans don't use it, this metaphor, which is taken from the term for a period of play

It wasn't until 1959—nearly two decades after naysayers argued otherwise—that experiments by Lyman Briggs, the director of the U.S. National Bureau of Standards at that time, seemed to end the discussion by proving the curveball did what its name claimed.

Even so, in 2009, there were still physicists who pointed out that while the pitch does dip, it doesn't alter its path as much as or in the manner we think it does. Of course, Dizzy Dean, who was one of baseball's great characters from the 1930s and 1940s, would have suffered none of these nuances if he were around today. He once said about curveball skeptics: "Go stand behind a tree, and I'll hit you with an optical illusion."

in cricket, describes a person who has enjoyed a good and/or meaningful life (e.g., "The recently deceased doctor had a good innings").

Screwball. Before it was a nickname for a daffy person, a genre of film comedy, or a pitch delivered by baseball players, a *screwball* was a term for a type of cricket throw that moved unexpectedly.

A sticky wicket. It's used more in Britain to portray a difficult situation but has devotees worldwide for its imagery. The wicket is another name for the playing surface, and sticky means slippery or wet (rather than tacky). Under those conditions, the batter faces a rough set of circumstances as the ball tends to bounce in unpredictable ways.

One thing is for certain: when people first started talking about ball games in America, they were talking baseball. The two terms (*ball game* and *baseball*) were used interchangeably by 1848, according to the *Dickson Baseball Dictionary*.

Baseball writers probably deserve credit for taking it one step further and coming up with *a different ball game* to describe a

Unexpected phrase from baseball: Catbird seat

The catbird's envious perch in the English language can be credited to two very successful men. The first is Walter Lanier "Red" Barber, one of baseball's great early broadcasters. During his stints on radio with the Brooklyn Dodgers (1939–1953) and the New York Yankees (1954–1966), the Mississippi-born Barber was known to infuse his work with homespun turns of phrase. One of his favorites was exclaiming that a player was in the *catbird seat* whenever he enjoyed a particularly advantageous situation. Why a catbird (a small species of bird with a warning chirp that sounds like a cat's meow) isn't wholly clear; one suggestion is they're particularly good at scoping out beneficial places to perch. But Barber would explain in his autobiography that he learned the idiom while getting beat in a card game in momentum shift or other dramatic change in a baseball contest. It showed up in game reports in 1913 and was regularly used on sports pages by the 1930s.

But after that, shifts in the sporting landscape create uncertainty. In the 1940s, talking about ball games was no longer the primary dominion of baseball. Journalists covering football began using the term far more often than their baseball colleagues in that decade (even some basketball stories began utilizing it).

Cincinnati. His opponent prevailed thanks to two face-down aces and explained he'd been in the catbird seat all along.

While Barber was offering up the expression to the masses by the early 1940s, it got its literary bona fides in 1942 from the famed short story writer James Thurber (author of, among many things, *The Secret Life of Walter Mitty*). That year, Thurber published a story named after the expression and even credited Barber for popularizing it. Wrote Thurber in *The Catbird Seat*: "'She must be a Dodger fan,' he had said, 'Red Barber announces the Dodger games over the radio and he uses those expressions—picked 'em up down South.'"

Today, it's so synonymous with being in an enviable position that when Natasha Trethewey was named U.S. Poet Laureate in 2012, she described the posting as "poetry's catbird seat."

As a result, when *a different ball game* (and the variation, *a whole new ball game*) became metaphorical in the 1960s and 1970s, it's not clear which sporting endeavor offered inspiration. Baseball may very well have been the driver, but an advertisement touting a "Whole New Ball Game" from a car dealership in the *Montana Standard* in 1960 suggests otherwise: when it came to illustrations to support that very early crossover reference, Copper City Chevrolet featured drawings of football players.

FAN

If ever there were a true fan of the game of baseball, it was Ted Sullivan. The Irish-born Sullivan occupied nearly every conceivable role in his beloved sport—player, manager, team owner, league founder, scout, agent, and marketer. Short of donning a mascot outfit, Sullivan did it all.

With that in mind, it makes sense that the word *fan* quite possibly began with him. That said, Sullivan was a storyteller, so pinning down the term's exact origin is difficult.

The most popular claim is that *fan*—as in a rabid supporter— entered our lexicon around 1882 as a shortened form of the term *fanatic*, which was already a tag for hardcore baseball groupies. Sullivan initially told reporters he first heard *fan* uttered in this manner by St. Louis Browns owner Chris Von der Ahe. The Germany-born entrepreneur possessed a thick accent, and the yarn goes that he had trouble saying *fanatic* so he reduced it to *fan*. Later, Sullivan would alter the story, nixing Von der Ahe and taking full credit for its creation.

But the *fanatic* root wasn't the only possible starting point. Perhaps, bored with that tale's plot line, Sullivan shifted the inspiration for the term in another retelling. He'd eventually say he coined it after he and one of his patrons, baseball magnate Charles Comiskey, were forced to listen to some men blabber on about baseball. Afterward, Sullivan dubbed them "fans," evoking images of their tongues wagging as fast as fans (in effect, using the fan analogy to refer to them as windbags).

Others have endorsed this connection to paper fans. Hall of Fame manager Connie Mack believed the word came from the handheld fans diehard baseball supporters used at early games. A final option is offered by the British: *fan* is derived from the *fancy*, which was a slang term for boxing that predated baseball (for more on the fancy, see "Floored" on page 111).

Perhaps the word was inspired by a critical mass of fanatics, paper fans, and the pugilist usage of *fancy*. It's a shame Sullivan isn't still around to offer a new narrative combining the three.

GET YOUR TURN AT BAT

Albert Einstein once said, "All that is valuable in human society depends upon the opportunity for development accorded the individual." Baseball's succinct shorthand for said opportunity is *getting your turn at bat*. It's one that resonates. Just look at George and Weezy, the main characters on the 1970s sitcom *The Jeffersons*, who moved from working-class circumstances to uptown, where George, in particular, was aiming for big-time success. As their theme song "Movin' On Up" unmistakably explained, these two battled to get to the big leagues and were finally getting their "turn at bat."

Major leaguers also yearn for those chances, though it wasn't always well defined when a player would get them. (In the case of the Jeffersons, it required years of living next to Archie Bunker

Unexpected word from baseball: Flake

Jackie Brandt was a journeyman outfielder who played parts of eleven Major League seasons from 1956–1967. He was also the planet's first official *flake*. A onetime All-Star and Gold Glove Award winner, Brandt's talents were overshadowed by his eccentricities. Among his kooky acts: he once hit a home run and supposedly slid into first, second, third, and home instead of jogging around the bases. It's also said that he once tried to do a backflip in an (unsuccessful) effort to avoid a tag.

Strange as he was, Brandt wouldn't have been the poster child for being flaky if not for another player's wit. Depending on who you believe, either an unnamed teammate with the San Francisco Giants in 1957 laid the nickname on him or a fellow member of the St. Louis Cardinals, Wally Moon, did it a year earlier. Either way, the rationale for the moniker was that his mind was so impermanent that his brains were flaking from his head. Some point to the fact that *flaky* was 1920s slang for a small packet of cocaine, but the direct and clear usage to describe Brandt (who proudly owned the title) suggests he's the source.

before they got their shot; if you don't know what I'm talking about, please study your classic television comedies.)

Baseball's original code dictated that hitters bat "in regular turn." But some saw that vague language as a loophole. Clubs often insisted that if the last out was made on the base paths, then the hitter who followed that runner in the lineup would lead off the next inning—even if he'd batted in the previous inning. This led to loads of confusion and was replaced in 1878 by a commitment to the type of sequential hitting we're accustomed to today.

While we now have a solid understanding of when you'll get your turn at bat, the order continues to matter greatly. All told, the first hitter usually gets 145 or more plate appearances per season than the person batting ninth.

GRANDSTANDING

Grandstanding—playing to the crowd—is a populist notion. While baseball had box seats where the rich sat in the days before luxury boxes, the wooden grandstands were the home of most regular fans. Describing a seating area as a grandstand was also used at horse racing tracks in England and America, but the idea of grandstanding by hamming up the action for the average paying spectators was purely ballpark language. Journalists were using it at the start of the twentieth century, and newspaper writers applied it to the grandest of populist-pandering folks—politicians—almost immediately.

In 1906, *The Washington Post* took it to describe the efforts of both Republican and Democratic U.S. Congressional campaigns. In a moment of understatement, the paper explained: "The appeal to the country as a whole is what may be called the public part of the work of the committees—'grandstanding' is the word employed to describe the process."

HIT AND RUN

The combination *hit and run* has become such a natural pairing. It's like a chocolate–peanut butter swirl of the English language—they go so well together. Among the various hit and runs: There's the driver who smacks another car or pedestrian and flees the scene; that usage existed by the mid-1920s. In 1950, *Time* magazine employed the expression to illustrate a type of picketing against AT&T where protesters would prevent workers from crossing their line and then move to another plant in the hopes of maximizing their efforts. Then there's the guy who bails after a one-night stand. Language experts have also picked it up to describe a quotation in an essay used without context or attribution. In fact, it's now unpacked for almost any instance wherein a grifter successfully commits a scam and departs without being caught.

Needless to say, it all started with the very real-world baseball strategy of a base runner sprinting to second base on the pitch and a batter trying to hit just about anything thrown to protect said runner and to take advantage of fielders moving to defend the steal. This maneuver, which dates back to the dawn of the sport, was fine-tuned by the Baltimore Orioles at the end of the 1890s. Their expertise led to the term getting wide play.

HOME RUN

Back in 2003, *USA Today* did a study ranking the hardest tasks in sports. It placed hitting a baseball at the top of the list. If you embrace the transitive postulate, then hitting a *home run* is the sporting world's biggest achievement. So when you're told in any endeavor that you've hit a home run—or its sister idioms, *hit* or *knocked it out of the park*—you've pretty much reached the apex of compliments.

Baseball did originally have difficulty settling on a definition for a home run. In the nineteenth century, calling something a home run often signaled any hit that allowed a player to scamper around the bases all the way home. Even if there were a *Bad News Bears* moment wherein fielders bobbled, missed, and errantly hucked the ball in unspeakable ways, the hitter who benefited would receive home-run plaudits. There were even some newspapers (ahem, *Atlanta Constitution*) that gave a home run to any player who happened to be on base when another hit a bases-rounding shot. So, if a runner on first scored on what we'd now call a homer, the paper proclaimed there were two home runs on the play.

By the twentieth century, leading baseball lights crystalized our current understanding of the term. Still, here's a little quibble about *hitting one out of the ballpark*: that statement really should mean smacking a ball beyond the confines of the whole stadium (rather than just reaching the outfield bleachers or hitting an inside-the-park homer). While truly hitting one out of the ballpark does happen at places like Wrigley Field and AT&T Park, surely that should be a step above hitting a garden-variety homer? Much to my disappointment, such a distinction is rarely, if ever, made.

INSIDE BASEBALL

When you literally look inside baseball (or at least the sport's instruction book), it's dense. The rules run more than fifty thousand words. Ask someone with a passing interest in the game to explain the infield fly rule, for example, and you'll invariably get a blank stare.

That should be enough of a road map for how the term *inside baseball* became synonymous with reveling in the minutiae only an expert could enjoy. And, yet, the path from the diamond to a synonym for intricate details wasn't quite as straightforward.

Inside baseball popped up as a description for a scientific approach to the game in the waning years of the nineteenth century. Teams trying new and innovative techniques earned the label. For example, the 1890s Baltimore Orioles, inventors of smacking the ball hard onto the turf in order to get a huge hop over infielders' heads (known as the Baltimore Chop), were an inside baseball team.

But in the opening decades of the twentieth century, the phrase took on a new meaning. Intrigue in baseball's back rooms was also going by the same term. For example, inside baseball status was conferred on acts like the commissioner's office banning White Sox players caught in the 1919 Black Sox scandal while allegedly protecting other superstars from potential gambling scandals.

Using the expression for this type of clandestine lever-pulling floated in the ether for a few decades until the 1950s, when journalists adapted it as a metaphor for political machinations. It was a Washington mainstay by 1954, when Senator Herman Welker of Idaho used it while discussing the ins and outs of specific phone records during the censure of Red Scare zealot Senator Joseph McCarthy.

OFF BASE

Getting *off base* may be a bad thing conversationally, but baseball has always allowed runners to do so. The big debate has been just how far they should stray. This discussion started way back in the 1880s, when speedster Mike "King" Kelly became famous for taking great liberties off first base before ultimately stealing second. (Geek note: Kelly was so great at stealing bases that a popular song of the day "Slide, Kelly, Slide" was written about him; he even endorsed a Slide, Kelly, Slide sled for snowy fun.) Still, others weren't so sure about such actions. Hall of Fame manager Connie Mack wrote in 1904 that straying too far from base was excessive and dangerous. These days, most believe that about ten to twelve feet (depending on your size) is optimal.

Strangely, another wrinkle to being off base in baseball was inspired by winter weather conditions. Believe it or not, baseball was occasionally played on ice with skates in the 1860s. Clearly, it was difficult to stop suddenly at the bases in this variation, so, as an accommodation, players skating to first were allowed to overshoot the base, according to baseball historian Peter Morris. The rule stuck on dry land as well.

As for *off base* meaning misguided or out of line, that usage was appearing in print in the mid-1930s. Though two variants— *off his base* (meaning eccentric or a bit kooky) and *caught off base* (being surprised)—predated it by at least a decade.

ON DECK

When a hitter is second up to bat in an inning we say he's *on deck*. Or in layman's terms, we use it to suggest "your turn is coming up next." But why a "deck"? The batter isn't taking practice swings on some sort of nicely varnished wooden area. The tiny town of Belfast, Maine, offers one of the best stories for the strange choice of words.

Located right on the sea, Belfast became a center of shipbuilding in the 1800s. Along with a love for the ocean, the locals had another passion—baseball. Despite its small size (fewer than seven thousand people), Belfast once even boasted having a minor league team.

Considering the village's feelings for the game of baseball, it was surely a really big deal when the famous Boston Red Stockings came to town in 1872 to play an exhibition game against a local club called the Pastimes. Lore tells us the event changed how we talk baseball.

Unexpected word from baseball: Jazz

The term for music's free-flowing all-American genre didn't start in New Orleans or even Chicago, two of the most important places for the early development of jazz. Nope, the name initially took hold in, of all places, California.

The first known written mention of the word *jazz* came in a 1912 *Los Angeles Times* article. A pitcher named Ben Henderson, who played for the Pacific Coast League's Portland Beavers, claimed he'd devised a fantastic pitch called a *jazz ball*. As Henderson would sport a 0–5 record that season (his last), it's doubtful the pitch mustered too much magic.

Instead, an influential sports writer named E. T. "Scoop" Gleeson brought fame to the name a year later. He was covering the San Francisco Seals, another Pacific Coast League team, at spring training in Sonoma County when he threw *jazz* into an article for the *San Francisco Bulletin* to reflect players competing with "pep, vim, [and] vigor." Gleeson, who years later would say he first heard the term

Each team had an announcer, and when the Red Stockings came to the plate, their scorer said the name of the first hitter batting. He then added that the batter would be followed next by two other hitters and gave each of their names. Looking to outdo his big-city competitor, the Belfast representative added a little

from a fellow reporter who applied it to describe the dice game craps, used the term constantly during the season.

Yet, even with Gleeson's affinity for jazz, luck deserves a lot of credit for bringing the word out of the baseball setting and into its current musical meaning. At the hotel where the San Francisco ball club was staying that spring, a group of musicians were on hand to entertain the guests. Led by Art Hickman, the band surely interacted with the players as well as reporters like Gleeson and heard the jazz lingo. While Hickman allegedly didn't like the word, the group's banjo player, Bert Kelly, loved it. A year later, he'd start his own group in Chicago, using the term to label his new band's sound.

By 1915, local Chicago papers were touting jazz, explaining how the word fit into the local music scene. "Blues is Jazz. Jazz is Blues," proclaimed the *Chicago Daily Tribune*. Publications in New Orleans, where most claim the style of music began, started using the term by 1916, and the word spread in smoky clubs around the United States, becoming a national phenomenon. Sadly for baseball, *jazz* quickly fizzled on ball fields.

flair to his presentation: he mentioned the name of the player at bat, but used seafaring terms for those coming after him. The second hitter was *on deck* (a term for being somewhat high up on a ship), and the third guy was *in the hold* (a lower spot on a boat). Over time, the unique phrasing stuck, with *in the hold* eventually changing to *in the hole*.

In all fairness, the use of *on deck* in this framework existed in at least one publication predating the Belfast moment, but it's equally possible that this application was novel to the announcer and spurred its spread via the Boston club. If so, it was the only win for the Belfast team that day as the local club lost on the field to Boston by a lopsided score of 35–1.

ON THE FLY

Catching a ball *on the fly* was a point of serious contention amid early baseball leaders—something that certainly brought the act to the attention of Americans and likely spurred its wider use in language. As odd as it might seem, the game's first rules made no distinction between snagging a ball on one hop and catching it cleanly in the air. Both constituted an out. In the late 1850s, one of baseball's original super clubs (the New York Knickerbockers) started narrowing the rule, cutting out one-hoppers as an automatic out. Such a change led to heated arguments. (Parties were so split that during this period, games were actually designated as "on the fly" or "on the bound" contests.)

No-bounce proponents pushed hard, suggesting that single-hop supporters were unmanly in allowing an out to occur in such a soft manner. Calling out one's manhood had its desired effect. In 1864, balls in fair territory were required to be plucked directly from the sky for a sure out. (Strangely, balls picked off one bounce in foul territory were still outs until the 1880s.)

One of the sport's first celebrity devotees, Walt Whitman, was familiar with this war of words. So much so, he took it as the basis for using *on the fly* to signify moving quickly with improvisation. "That has mainly been my method: I have caught much on the fly: things as they come and go—on the spur of the moment," he said in the 1880s. As author Ed Folsom put it in his book *Walt Whitman's Native Representations*, Whitman was "attracted to baseball metaphors for their colorful, direct, and simple expressiveness," and *on the fly* was one such example.

OUT IN LEFT FIELD

You can just hear Jerry Seinfeld (circa 1996) asking the question, "What's the deal with being *out in left field*? Why not *out in right field*, where you're supposed to stick the egghead?"

Beyond whatever punchline the famed comedian would have offered, there are a few explanations for the source of this idiom, which in the modern vernacular suggests being an oddball or a bit out of step.

One claim focuses on Chicago's old West Side Grounds, where the Cubs played from 1893–1915. The stadium's left field was supposedly located just behind the city's Neuropsychiatric Institute, which housed off-kilter patients. So, the innuendo came from being near a mental hospital. A plaque close to the old stadium's location was erected in 2008 to support this claim. (The problem: The phrase doesn't appear to have been commonly voiced until the mid-1900s—long after the West Side Grounds were a distant memory.)

Another possibility comes from New York Yankees' lore. Only eccentric folks, this line of thinking goes, would choose to sit in Yankee Stadium's left field bleachers because doing so provided the worst view of the game's best player—right-fielder Babe Ruth. (Again, the timing might not be right on this one.)

Some suggest the key is in the use of *left*, as the left side has a historically symbolic connection with gawkiness, clumsiness, or even subversive proclivities (as a left-hander, I only grudgingly offer this one).

An additional entrant hones in on the fact that left-fielders were actually far out there. Supposedly, left-fielders used to play deeper than other outfielders because right-handed sluggers tended to smack the ball farther to that area.

Final choice: The sun blinded right-fielders at big-league parks, meaning players out there were the strongest corner outfield defenders; hence, being *out in left field* was a put-down.

The music business may have developed the similarly constructed term *out of left field* for something that comes as a complete surprise. That variation, according to a 1949 book, arose in Tin Pan Alley during the early twentieth century. The author, Arnold Shaw, claimed the baseball-inspired expression, "that was a hit out of left field" was used for an unexpectedly successful result. Then again, it may have simply been shocking that something positive would come out of left field, where the crazies—at least in an idiomatic sense—lived.

PINCH-HIT

When you *pinch-hit* for someone at work, no doubt, you want to do your best. But you don't expect it to be a white-knuckle ride. Yet, in original baseball terms, pinch-hitting came with stress levels at the top of the tension spectrum.

During the first decade of the twentieth century, hitting in a "pinch" situation had nothing to do with substitutions. It meant coming to bat in a contest's most nerve-wracking juncture—whenever that might be. For example, in 1900, a local newspaper in Fort Wayne, Indiana, portrayed the town's everyday third baseman Charlie Babb as a "pinch" hitter for his regular clutch base hits.

The explanation for this usage lies in the history of the word *pinch*. Beginning in the fifteenth century, it was used in England to describe "an instance, occasion, or time of special difficulty," according to the *Oxford English Dictionary*. Major writers were still using that definition around the time baseball appropriated the term. Famed author Robert Louis Stevenson, for instance, included the phrase *in a pinch* to express a tough moment in his 1888 novel *The Black Arrow*.

Three years later, baseball manager Patsy Tebeau trailblazed when he replaced the pitcher in his Cleveland Spiders' lineup with a better batter from the bench. It led to a four-run outburst against the Chicago Cubs. Alas, Tebeau hadn't fully considered this new strategy and was left without a regular pitcher. The result: His club lost anyway.

Describing Tebeau's tactic as "bringing in a pinch hitter" didn't catch on until around 1905, when Hall of Fame manager John McGraw made the maneuver a relatively accepted occurrence. Not long after, popular culture embraced it as well. A 1917 silent film called *The Pinch Hitter* told the story of a country boy who becomes a hero when he gets a shot at pinch-hitting. For acts off the diamond, to pinch-hit (as in "the musical's understudy pinch-hit for the sick starlet") had crossed over by 1914.

Within the next couple of decades, *going to bat* for someone emerged as well. While in baseball parlance, the phrase could be used interchangeably with pinch-hit, the colloquial applications diverged. Pinch-hitting simply represented serving as a substitute, while going to bat for another reflected really make an effort on another's behalf.

One final variation to consider: if you're going to bat for a group on a pretty onerous task (or simply accepting a horrible assignment no one else will endure), you can be said to be *taking one for the team*. A reference to this self-sacrifice can be found in a 1969 amateur baseball game report about a player in Texas willing to get hit by a pitch for the greater good of his club. By the early 1970s, other sports were using it (a 1973 mention exists in a National Hockey League game report). Idiomatically, it was popping up by 1977.

PLAY BALL

There is some long-forgotten umpire who deserves a proverbial tip of the cap for introducing *play ball*. The original rules of baseball required the ump to shout an unfussy "Play" to start a game, but at some point in baseball's first decade or so, some innovative soul changed it to "Play ball" and it stuck.

The combination of *play* and *ball* preceded baseball, but the general meaning of cooperating with someone on an initiative almost certainly comes from the sport. The reason: timing. The phrase as we know it first popped up in print in 1903, according to the *Oxford English Dictionary*. By that point, the overwhelmingly central ball game in America was baseball and the phrase was synonymous with it.

The idiom's tougher cousin—*to play hardball*—wasn't popularly used to represent being unyielding or pushy in dealings until the 1970s. The word *hardball* did enter the baseball lexicon in the 1880s, most likely to distinguish the sport's orb from the sphere used in softball.

RAIN CHECK

Customer satisfaction hasn't always been at the top of baseball's business plan (fans won't likely soon forget the eight work stoppages between 1972 and 1994). Nevertheless, in 1890, the National League thoughtfully added the requirement for *rain checks* to its constitution as a way to guarantee spectators got what they'd paid for. If you went to a game and inclement weather prevented it from reaching an official completion, you could come back and see another contest.

While the practice hit the big time with the National League, various teams from New Orleans to Toledo had already been providing this courtesy during the decade before. New Orleans Pelicans' owner Abe Powell claimed he created a physically reusable ticket stub (aka a "rain check") for the paying clientele in the late 1880s. Regrettably, there was no touchy-feely reason for his invention. He just grew tired of freeloaders trying to sneak in claiming they'd been at a rained-out match.

If Abe or other baseball leaders did truly invent the rain check, it spread quickly. In 1887, a *Detroit Free Press* article told the story of a shoe-shiner who offered rain checks, and in 1903 the *Daily Kennebec Journal* in Augusta, Maine, spun the phrase deftly for figurative purposes. "If you expect to do anything to make people remember you, it is time to get at it," the article extolled—"St. Peter isn't going to issue any rain checks."

RIGHT OFF THE BAT

No matter how quickly you make a suggestion *right off the bat*, it won't match the speed of a real ball smacked by some lumber. At the Major League level, balls can reach an exit velocity as high as 120 miles per hour following contact. And while you can look silly if you're too quick with a right-off-the-bat statement, you're not nearly in the same danger as a pitcher facing a line drive right off a hitter's bat. The reaction time for such a shot can be less than four tenths of a second.

Americans cottoned to the phrase in the early days of baseball. A reference pops up in the 1869 book *Letters of Peregrin Pickle*

Rounding the bases: Metaphors for getting it on

It's an early teenage rite of passage—or at least it used to be—to learn the sexual meaning for each base. Decades ago, it started at first base with a kiss and got more physically intimate as you made your way around the diamond to the almighty grail of home. (Apparently, the value of some of the bases have been ratcheted up over the years.)

The connection between sprinting around the bases, dirt in your cleats and sweat pouring down your face, doesn't seem like an obvious starting point for this metaphor (okay, maybe the sweating part). So how did this sexual code language become a staple for junior high school conversation?

The key may be at first base. Beginning in the early part of the twentieth century, *getting to first base* had a broader meaning. It generally reflected taking the initial step toward just about anything. (Example: "Now that the stove is installed, we've finally gotten to first base on this kitchen remodel.")

by George P. Upton. In contemplating "base-ballists," he writes, "The Devil is not only a hard hitter with the bat, but he is a quick fielder, and he will pick a soul right off the bat of one of these soft muscle men."

A more layman's usage can be found in a January 1900 article in the *New Albany* (Indiana) *Evening Tribune*. Discussing U.S.

This made perfect sense, as first base is the preliminary achievement on a baseball player's quest to score a run.

With this background, writers in the 1930s began talking about getting to first base in relationships (these were innocent days, so sex wasn't even in the equation). A 1939 article in the *Hammond* (Indiana) *Times*, for example, addressed a boy's chances of getting a date if he crassly made a randy remark to a female stranger. "If you're one of them," explained the story's writer, "please change because you aren't getting to first base with us. You're just being rude."

Over time, this usage gained momentum and more explicit significance. While it was already common by the 1970s, rounding the metaphorical bases reached iconic standing when Meatloaf used it in his 1977 rock anthem "Paradise by the Dashboard Light." In the song, New York Yankees great Phil Rizzuto famously contributed allusions to loving and the bases but publicly claimed he was completely unaware of the sexual implications. If so, he was the only one.

senators getting to work quickly upon their return from hiatus, the journalist wrote, they "began business 'right off the bat' as the baseball enthusiast would say."

ROOT

One thing we know about early baseball followers—they took their teams seriously. In language, that intensity is evident in terms like *fan* (see page 18) and *root* (as in "I root for the Red Sox"). To understand the importance of *root*, consider baseball's most iconic song: "Take Me Out to the Ball Game." You don't cheer, cheer, cheer for your club; you root, root, root for the home team.

The most popular explanation comes from the botanical world. Baseball buffs were metaphorically rooted to their club of choice and the noun *rooters* sprang from there (with their primary action being *rooting*). There's an elegance to this explanation because *rooted* has by and large been used as a representation for a strong link or attachment to another since at least the seventeenth century.

A more detailed theory contemplates the foot stamping that spectators often did in stadiums to back their team. This noisy effort could look as if the rooters were digging holes with their shoes or, to put it another way, rooting with their feet. Another old definition that potentially gave inspiration is *to work or study hard*. No doubt, a good session of rooting requires some sweat of the brow.

STEP UP TO THE PLATE

The easy part of this idiom is understanding why *stepping up to the plate* is a big deal. Generally speaking, it's that moment when an individual takes his or her turn at an activity. But, implicitly, it's more than that—it's when a person enters the spotlight looking to achieve glory or, as Teddy Roosevelt said about the arena, to fail "while daring greatly."

Stepping up to the plate in an actual game is no different: the batter stands alone in a one-on-one clash with the pitcher. The upshot: Entering the batter's box works perfectly as a metaphor. Still, there's an obvious hiccup in the phrase. Anybody who has ever been to a baseball game can tell you that home plate looks nothing like, well, a plate (you know, as in the place for mashed potatoes and steak).

What's up with that?

To find an answer, you have to start way back in 1845. Instead of a five-sided slab of rubber, home was a flat, circular piece of iron painted white, approximately a foot in diameter. The object, which we now know colloquially as *the dish* because of that original design, could have been plucked from a working-class kitchen (save the leaden paint). But, despite its culinary benefits, the plate was dangerous for sliding purposes (hadn't these people heard of tetanus?), so improvements were made over the years. In 1869, the round form was replaced by a twelve-inch square with points directed at the pitcher and the catcher. A marble slab came into vogue in 1872, before everyone finally thought safety first and went with rubber in 1885.

The up-to-date version was installed in 1900 to make it easier for umpires to recognize balls and strikes. Its resemblance to a house—or in a baseball sense, home—is mere coincidence.

The whole idea of a *strike out*—in baseball terms—is a bit of an oxymoron. After all, the climactic third strike in a strike out doesn't even involve striking the ball. (If you want to get picky, a foul tip can lead to a strike out, but there's nothing striking about that contact.) Even more baffling, in modern baseball, you can avoid making any attempt to strike a ball and still strike out.

A brief game changer: Softball

No offense to softball players, but if you're enjoying the game's slow-pitch variety in a recreational setting, hitting a leisurely tossed grapefruit-sized projectile isn't one of sports' most difficult tasks. Still, that very activity was once a central part of the American workplace. Back in the second half of the twentieth century, before the proliferation of alt-kitschy team sports (not long ago, no self-respecting adult was playing kick ball), company softball teams were extremely common throughout the United States.

So, when journalists in the early 1970s started calling easy queries lobbed toward a politician *softball questions*, it just made sense. Though slow-pitch softball has seen a decline, the phrase has persisted and migrated from elected officials to celebrities and athletes who love taking a swing at those simple requests for information.

Some sense of how we got to this seeming contradiction can be found in baseball's original rules. The New York Knickerbockers, who memorialized the sport's first how-to instructions in 1845, really liked the word *strike*. Batters were called *strikers* and the verb *to strike* shows up a number of times in the original twenty laws. So, not surprisingly, *strike*—as in *to hit*—was going to get into the game's lexicon.

At the same time, the Knickerbocker rules didn't create a system for balls and strikes. In other words, a hitter couldn't get out without at least attempting to strike the ball (if he didn't swing, the pitcher would just keep throwing until he did).

This surely led to some linguistic difficulty. Describing an out built on a failed effort to strike a baseball isn't easy to do in a pithy manner (*out by missed strike* or *strike-less out* both feel a bit clunky). Perhaps, this led to the truncated *strike out*. It's worth noting the phrase *to strike out* was used in this period outside of sports with different meanings, ranging from canceling something with the stroke of a pen to embarking on a new path. Possibly familiarity with one of these definitions helped spur the baseball usage.

In 1864, the concept of the strike zone was added to the rules. From then on, an umpire was empowered to decide if a pitch was a ball or a strike when a hitter didn't attempt to hit the ball. But by that point, *strike out* was already part of the game's language, thus starting it on the path to representing failing at everything from dating to buying a food processor on eBay.

SWINGING FOR THE FENCES

Most baseball players will tell you that trying to hit a home run won't lead to that desired result; those blasts just come as a product of good overall hitting. As Hall of Famer Cal Ripken Jr. succinctly explained in his autobiography, *The Only Way I Know*, "If I deliberately try to hit a home run, I don't."

So are we setting people up for disaster when we encourage them to *swing for the fences*? It depends on whom you're asking. Babe Ruth appeared to be aiming for the next zip code every time he came to bat and once quipped, "If I'd tried for them dinky singles, I could've batted around six hundred." (For stat hounds, even with his homer approach, the Yankees right-fielder owned a lofty career .342 batting average to go along with his 714 lifetime home runs.)

Spitballing: Baseball or back-of-the-classroom behavior?

Wouldn't it be a lot of fun if rather than saying, "Let's do some *spitballing* for the new advertising campaign," we encouraged some *cuspidor curving* or *aqueous tossing*? Those are just two examples of the more than thirty-five synonyms for the sneaky pitch known as the *spitball*. Requiring a liberal dose of saliva or other foreign substance to send a ball moving in all sorts of unexpected ways, the pitch came into baseball vogue in 1904 and 1905. It was so devastating in its ability to get batters out that leagues began outlawing it by 1918. (Of course, as an illegal option, it remains in some hurlers' repertoire to this day.)

While the spitball's lawful rise and fall was quick, the vernacular meaning—throwing out off-the-top-of-the-head

Broadly speaking, Ruth's strategy as a hitter may have been a bit more nuanced than just going for the fences every time. "I swing as hard as I can, and I try to swing right through the ball," he said.

If you want to take Ruth's advice, maybe the idiom should be *swing as hard as you can right through the ball*. (There is the phrase *swinging from your heels*, which does get a bit technical in describing taking a wildly big—and undoubtedly ill-advised— hack for the fences on the field or in life.) Still, there's something graceful about swinging for the fences that signifies going for the

suggestions in a discussion—has been far more enduring. The only question is whether it was spurred by baseball or by kids who wad up paper in their mouth to create projectiles (which, arguably, is also a sport). This latter form of spitballing, in both practice and language, had showed up by 1846, far predating its baseball debut.

We do know the term in its idiomatic sense was regularly uttered by the mid-twentieth century. In 1977, *New York Times* language writer William Safire argued that the erratic character of a pitcher's spitball was the jumping-off point for this speculative form of brainstorming. But the haphazard nature of youthful spitballing is also a legit contender. On balance, the thought of shooting wet paper to see if it sticks probably lines up better with this definition.

greatest result. The phrase existed in the 1920s in the baseball milieu and was used for all occasions by the 1950s.

SWITCH-HITTER

Little did Bob Ferguson know that a shift from the right side of the batter's box to the left on June 14, 1870, would be the first step in inspiring a term for bisexuality. All Ferguson figured was he wanted to thoroughly rattle the other team.

The details behind the first well-known decision to switch-hit were quite dramatic. Ferguson's Brooklyn Atlantics were playing the Cincinnati Red Stockings—a club in the midst of a mind-boggling eighty-nine-game winning streak. The Atlantics had forced the game into extra innings when Ferguson came to the plate trailing the dominant Cincinnati club.

Normally a right-hander, he shocked everyone by stepping up as a lefty. The move was supposedly to unnerve the opposition and to help him avoid hitting the ball to the Red Stockings' deft shortstop George Wright. It worked. Ferguson pulled the ball toward the first baseman, and it scooted into the outfield to score the tying run. The Atlantics would quickly tally another run to win, and the heroics of switch-hitting became known nationwide.

It's unclear whether the designation *switch-hitter* was immediately applied to Ferguson. Still, the term had entered print by the 1920s. Later, the phrase fit neatly into the sexual awakening of the 1960s. Switch-hitter was already defined in 1960 as "a bisexual person" by the *Dictionary of American Slang*. This meaning was so mainstream by 1975 that Ann Landers used it in one of her advice columns discussing bisexuality that year: "Greg is bisexual. His preference may change again from guys to girls, or he might be a switch-hitter for the rest of his life."

Chapter 2

BASKETBALL

"If it makes money, then no harm, no foul."

—Director James Cameron the day his megabudgeted
blockbuster *Titanic* was released

BALLER

Even if you're not a connoisseur of rap or hip-hop, you've probably at least heard of the term *baller*. The list of artists who have discussed the baller lifestyle include such luminaries as 2Pac, Kanye West, Drake, Nicki Minaj, P. Diddy, Ice Cube, Jay-Z, and Eminem.

If that's not your bag, here's a concise explainer: a baller is a person who's risen to the big-time, living lavishly and spending freely (and, in some cases, acquiring wealth from illegal pursuits). The slang has been in place since at least the start of the 1990s.

As for where the word itself comes from, it existed in the nineteenth century and early twentieth century for a variety of athletes who played games that feature spheres such as soccer, baseball, cricket, and football.

But it was the swinging lifestyle of basketball players that directly gave rise to this nonsporty application. As the *Oxford English Dictionary* puts it—in its typical scholarly fashion—the term references "the perceived tendency of successful basketball players to spend ostentatiously."

The *OED* is not alone in this observation. In 2004, when a video game called *NBA Ballers* was released, the *Los Angeles Times* echoed the high-flying reputation. "Like many an NBA player," a reviewer wrote, "*NBA Ballers* seems deeply concerned about acquiring fancy wheels and bling bling. Style is everything here—and court performance is just the means to get it."

FULL-COURT PRESS

When you see the all-out pressure of a *full-court press* in a basketball game, it's easy to identify. What's not as easy is pinpointing who created and named this smothering pressure defense.

Wichita State University has bestowed its former coach Gene Johnson with the honor, but numerous sources say John McLendon, one of the game's great innovators, is the man deserving the props. Others stump for New Mexico high school coach Ralph Tasker or St. Ambrose (Iowa) University's Bob Duax. It's likely they all deserve some pioneering repute with Johnson and McLendon out front.

Johnson, who followed up his stint with Wichita State by running a famous amateur team in the mid-1930s called the McPherson Globe Refiners, believed he played a role in nurturing the defensive style. But in a June 25, 1972, interview with the *Hutchinson* (Kansas) *News*, he disclaimed his title as the originator. Instead, he credited an unnamed team in Mexico that once pressed his Refiners club for inspiring him.

McLendon was a massive success at universities like North Carolina Central and Tennessee State as well as being the first African American to serve as a head coach in professional basketball. He unquestionably revolutionized an up-tempo style that included the all-court press, though it's unclear if he did it first.

Regardless, the efforts of these groundbreaking coaches led to the full-court press becoming commonplace in the 1950s. As *Sports Illustrated* pointed out in a 1965 article, a number of NCAA national championship teams in the 1950s like University of Kansas (1952), University of San Francisco (1955 and 1956), and University of California–Berkeley (1959) used it.

Who was the first to coin *full-court press* to represent the strategy? All we know is that it was in print by the late 1940s. In reaching idiomatic prominence as a saying for a stifling attack, it received an unexpected—and doubtless unwelcomed— boost from President Richard Nixon in 1974. That year, White House recordings (aka the Watergate tapes) were released with the president talking about using a "full-court press" in his dubious dealings.

GOING ONE-ON-ONE

What would James Naismith, inventor of basketball, think about people *going one-on-one* in his beloved sport?

One fact is certain: he wasn't too bothered about team size when he formulated the game. His famous original thirteen rules didn't say anything about how many players were required. The first basketball scrimmage Naismith ever organized featured nine-on-nine. In the sport's initial handful of years, the custom was to simply split a group of participants in half and have them compete. (Naismith even told a story of a teacher at Cornell University who set up a match featuring fifty members to a side.) The rules didn't clearly insist on five players on the court per team until 1897, six years after basketball's genesis.

Yet, even with Naismith's initial flexibility, it's unlikely he would have fancied the one-on-one version of his creation. In his book *Basketball: Its Origin and Development*, Naismith outlined what he hoped participants of his sport would achieve. In particular, he called for cooperation and self-sacrifice. Neither attribute is easily honed in a game of one-on-one.

But the ease with which basketball could be distilled into a two-person game was undeniable. Early on, coaches relied on drills featuring individual players matching up to improve skills, and by the 1930s, the term *one-on-one* was routinely applied to such exercises (later *one-on-one* developed meaning in football when a defender was tasked with covering an offensive player without any additional help). While people undoubtedly played one-on-one basketball games from the sport's youthful days, the idea of one-on-one basketball tournaments proliferated after World War II.

It picked up momentum as a general phrase in the 1970s. During the Democratic presidential primaries in 1972, a reporter pointed out that U.S. Senator Hubert Humphrey was "delighted with a chance to go one-on-one against" fellow senator and eventual nominee George McGovern in a debate.

HOME COURT ADVANTAGE

A staple bar topic—after a few drinks—is the value of *home court advantage* in sports. The phrase sprung from college and high school basketball writers who, by the 1920s, were touting its role in games. Newspapers from Syracuse, New York, to El Paso, Texas, took note of the upside of playing on your home court during that decade, and, if you saw the movie *Hoosiers*, it's hard to deny that competing in your own peculiar version of a gym with the whole town rooting for you can have a positive effect.

Still, everyone has an opinion. One newswire reporter in 1963 said that the bump really came from "home officiating advantage" as the locals were able to bring out (or at least influence) referees who were sympathetic to their cause. A cynical 1981 letter writer to the *New York Times* claimed home court advantage was a conspiracy to help the hosting team perform well enough to improve their financial bottom line.

In 1941, a reporter out of Dallas somehow put a value on the home court advantage. It "is usually worth at least five points in basketball," he wrote authoritatively. One guy who disagreed with this perspective was former New Jersey Nets coach Stan Albeck. In 1984, he succinctly explained: "It doesn't mean [expletive]."

Sorry, Stan, but if you talk to the number crunchers, home court advantage does mean [expletive]. You can check out studies in such highfalutin periodicals as the *Journal of Applied Social Psychology* and *Current Directions in Psychological Science* for backup.

Folks in other fields didn't need such scientific support before extolling the impact of home court advantage. The phrase was being used in a legal sense in the 1970s (the double meaning for *court* was probably too hard to pass up). Business writers also liked it. A 1978 book called *How to Get the Upper Hand: Simple Techniques You Can Use to Win the Battles of Everyday Life* devoted a section to the value of controlling venue in all situations. The chapter was "Home Court Advantage."

One final point worth noting: the similar *home field advantage* had also entered sports parlance by the 1920s. Football writers used it often, but baseball—with its numerous quirky stadiums (think, Fenway Park)—also surely nudged that one along to nonathletic use.

IN YOUR FACE

Though it might be getting a bit worn, *in your face* remains a brash way to say, "I got the better of you." Just ask the hip-hop duo Insane Clown Posse, who repeated it eighteen times in their 2006 song "In Yo Face."

The phrase got its start on urban blacktop basketball courts and was regularly bandied about on playgrounds by the 1970s. (A 1992 *New York Times* letter to the editor claimed it had already

Unexpected phrase from basketball: My bad

Manute Bol's story is so improbable. A Dinka tribesman who never played basketball until his late teens, Bol became a National Basketball Association regular for the better part of a decade. Even more unbelievable: the 7'7" center, who spoke no English when he arrived in the United States in 1983 as a twenty-year-old, contributed to the English language by popularizing *my bad*, which has become a mainstay for minor mistake makers throughout America.

Still learning the game—and the language—while playing at his sport's highest level in the mid-1980s, Bol understandably struggled with some words. This hurdle likely led him to say *my bad* instead of *my fault* when he made a mistake on the court.

While some language experts believe the phrase may date back to the 1940s jazz culture, or existed in some basketball pockets before Bol, a significant number of stories in 1989 give Bol credit for bringing it to the NBA. At the least, he gave the phrase the boost that propelled it into general conversation. (I'm pretty sure that I, for one, use it on a daily basis.)

Beyond his work in the NBA, Bol was known as a sincere humanitarian and a freedom fighter for those devastated by civil strife in Sudan. When it came to the issues that really mattered, Bol, who passed away in 2010 at the age of forty-seven, had no reason ever to say *my bad*.

been thrown around during 1950s inner-city pickup basketball games in Baltimore.)

In print, author Charles Rosen used it in a 1975 book he cowrote with basketball coaching great Phil Jackson called *Maverick: More Than a Game*. He brought it out again for a novel he published the following year called *A Mile Above the Rim*. In 1980, it was not only part of the title, but also a defined term in *The In-Your-Face Basketball Book*, which investigated the sport's greatest pickup game spots across America.

In your face is a "phrase to be uttered after making a shot or defensive play that humiliates an opponent," authors Chuck Wielgus and Alexander Wolf explained.

The idea behind *in your face* resonated in the rap music community with MCs transforming it in the 1980s and 1990s into a broader meaning—being bold, provocative, aggressive, or up close and personal. It's a move the Insane Clown Posse surely appreciated.

NO HARM, NO FOUL

Trained as a doctor, Hall of Fame basketball coach Henry Clifford Carlson carried his scientific education into his career in sports. The Hippocratic Oath requires physicians to do no harm, and Carlson, who was a well-known coach at the University of Pittsburgh, put that concept to the test in basketball when he studied the personal foul. It was a course of inquiry that led him to becoming an early user of the phrase *no harm, no foul*.

In 1954, a year after his final season at Pitt, Carlson (nicknamed "Doc") broke down the fouling issue in his beloved game. As he saw it, there were three categories of violations: negligible, questionable, and unquestionable. Doc argued that if the negligible types were ignored, the total number of fouls would decrease by 30 percent, leading to a faster, more exciting brand of the sport.

"In Dr. Carlson's opinion, if the rule 'no harm, no foul' were followed, a great game would be made greater," the *News* in Newport, Rhode Island, reported in October 1954. Later that year, the *Pittsburgh Post-Gazette* would credit Carlson with first proposing this no harm, no foul philosophy.

Now Carlson may have been the expression's initial high-profile apostle, but some recognition for its ubiquity has to go to the Los Angeles Lakers' longtime broadcaster Francis "Chick" Hearn (see "Slam dunk" below). Hearn picked up the catchy phrase and wielded it so often that many incorrectly credit him with its creation.

Nonetheless, Hearn was the Lakers' broadcaster from 1961 to 2002, so he was well positioned to line up *no harm, no foul* for its eventual transition off the hard court.

SLAM DUNK

Basketball has an abundance of talkers. Just check out Shaquille O'Neal's Twitter feed or Charles Barkley's website for some examples. But for all the big gabbers in the sport's history, the game's greatest voice never took a shot or pulled down a rebound in his career. His name was Chick Hearn.

As the Los Angeles Lakers longtime broadcaster, Hearn called an astounding 3,338 consecutive games between 1965 and his death in 2002. His strategy on the air was to speak quickly but clearly. But his greatest talent was popularizing phrases and terms.

When a poor shot was made, he'd lament that the player *threw up a brick* or if the effort completely missed the rim, he was the first to call it an *air ball*. Other terms included the *charity stripe* for the free throw line, a *dribble drive* for when a player finessed his way to the basket while dribbling, and a *ticky tack foul* for an overzealous call by the referee (for another example of his etymological influence, see "No harm, no foul" on page 50).

But for all his linguistic flair, Hearn's greatest contribution to everyday language was the *slam dunk*. The idea of stuffing the ball through the basket was initially deemed a violent and uncivilized

Unexpected phrase from basketball: Go-to guy

The first *go-to guy* we know of—at least in the written word—was a basketball player named Derek Smith. A college star at the University of Louisville, Smith had some good stretches in his nine-year, five-team National Basketball Association career, and his 1984–1985 campaign with the Los Angeles Clippers was one such period. His coach Don Chaney took notice.

"Derek is one of my go-to guys—players who want the ball in crucial situations," he told United Press International on April 4, 1985. The same day, Chaney also told a Southern California paper called the *Daily Breeze* that Smith had "become our 'go-to' guy."

The go-to concept was clearly in circulation elsewhere around the same time. The same day Chaney was giving Smith the go-to guy love, a *Washington Post* article had a high act, so much so that from 1967–1976, the NCAA banned the move from its games.

Luckily for Hearn (and the English language), his Lakers had just the right player to be the muse for his grandiose expression. At 7'1″, Wilt Chamberlain didn't have too much difficulty rising above the basket and forcefully depositing the ball into the net. He joined the Lakers for the 1968–1969 season, and Hearn uttered the famed slam dunk exhortation early in that campaign; by the season's mid-point, local newspapers had picked up on the

school coach calling future NBA stalwart Sherman Douglas "the go-to man."

Even if Smith or our first go-to man Douglas were not the absolute pioneers, lauding players on the hardwood surely led to the phrase's popularity. While a sprinkling of football players was labeled go-to guys in this period, late 1980s references were dominated by basketball stars getting the title. Case in point: Journalist Tony Kornheiser, who would go on to TV fame on ESPN, was an early adopter, using it in at least two articles on basketball in 1988. In December that year, he wrote in the *Washington Post*: "All the better teams in the NBA have at least one 'go-to guy,' someone they depend on either to get the bucket or get fouled when they need two points."

By the 1990s, the NBA was not alone—companies outside the sports realm were also describing employees who they could rely on in the crunch as go-to guys.

phrase and were including it in their stories. (All that said, it's worth noting that Hearn's slam dunk was a twist on the slightly more benign term *dunk shot*, which had been around in print since at least 1935.)

In the mid-1970s, the *slam dunk* began meaning "a sure thing" in everyday speech. Evidently, somebody forgot to tell greats like Michael Jordan, Kobe Bryant, and LeBron James, who have all endured embarrassing missed dunks in their careers.

Chapter 3

FOOTBALL

**"[Americans] know how to enthuse, know how
to sell a film, know how to run with the ball."**

—Director John Schlesinger (*Midnight Cowboy*)

ARMCHAIR QUARTERBACK

The rise of football on television has led to the development of many things, including bad pizza commercials, Super Bowl parties, those weird robot graphics on Fox TV, and *armchair quarterbacks*. It's not that we haven't had second-guessing fans since the dawn of the sport, but the idiom didn't exist until those folks properly settled into their Barcaloungers with cold beers in hand.

There was a go-to term for these types before the game became, for many, primarily a televised experience. Those who went to games and questioned coaching decisions were called *grandstand quarterbacks* beginning in the 1920s.

Radio broadcasts started in 1921, and the first televised game took place in 1938, although it wasn't until the 1950s that both college and professional contests became regular programming. Not surprisingly, during that decade, the home-dwelling version of the grandstand quarterback started becoming a popular label. *Armchair quarterback* gained traction as a name for an opinionated nonexpert from all walks of life in the 1970s. A real world example: An assistant police chief in a March 1971 edition of the *Salt Lake City Tribune* likened juries to "the armchair quarterback who calls all the right plays with the benefit of hindsight."

BLINDSIDED

Football Hall of Fame linebacker Lawrence Taylor has never lacked ego. When it comes to the *blind side* in football (that dangerous area the quarterback can't see behind his back when he drops back to pass), Taylor claims his talents led to the term.

"It wasn't really called the blind side when I came into the league [in 1981]," Taylor told author Michael Lewis for the book *The Blind Side*. "It was called the right side. It became the blind side after I started knocking people's heads off."

With all due respect to Taylor, *blind side* is a very old expression dating back to the 1600s that broadly describes "the unguarded, weak, or assailable side of a person or thing," according to the *Oxford English Dictionary*. It was ready-made for football via rugby: when football was first developed, rugby was already using the *blind side* as jargon for the area of a scrum opposite where the main line of opposing backs were located. References to the term in football can be found in the 1920s, though considering the sport's rugby ties, the phrase was probably used even earlier.

While blind side wasn't a football (or Taylor) creation, the gridiron did develop the verb *to blindside*. Newspapers were using this term in the early 1960s. Not long after, an assortment of publications quoted individuals equating getting hit off the field to being blindsided as a football player. By the 1970s, people were brandishing the metaphorical *blindside* when receiving—or giving—an unwelcome surprise.

CALLING AN AUDIBLE

Audible, as in detectable by the ear, dates back to the fifteenth century. But in the twentieth century, football gave the term a new use: in the early 1950s, the phrase *calling an audible* described a quarterback changing the plan at the line of scrimmage.

Though it's widely embraced today, the strategy wasn't always a favorite of big-name coaches. For instance, Paul Brown, a Hall of Famer who famously ran all aspects of his teams, allegedly didn't embrace quarterback improvisation. A former Brown assistant told a journalist in 1969, "Well . . . the guy sending in the play is the head coach, the general manager, and the principal voting owner. This is not an easy situation to audibilize."

If Brown cared deeply about language, he might also have been flummoxed by the use of the word *audible*. After all, *calling a change* would have been a clearer descriptor. And, using *calling* and *audible* together seems redundant (could someone make a vocal call that wasn't audible?).

One possible explanation for the combo was a popular World War II application of the word *audible*. The phrase *audible signal* was often used to describe earsplitting air-raid sirens that regularly bellowed in preparation for bombings that, thankfully, never occurred in the continental United States. Post-war football coaches may have co-opted that construction, using *calling an audible* to convey loudly getting your teammates' attention for a last-minute shift.

The use of this saying for any sort of last-minute switch was in play by the 1960s. In July 1969, *Sports Illustrated* ran an ad in the *New York Times* encouraging companies to buy advertisements in its publication. "If your advertising isn't programmed for sports," the magazine proclaimed, "there's still time to call an audible— and call SI."

CHEERLEADER

In his celebrated two-volume opus *Democracy in America*, Alexis de Tocqueville wrote: "Here and there, in the midst of American society, you meet with men, full of a fanatical and almost wild enthusiasm, which hardly exists in Europe." One can only imagine what de Tocqueville might have said if he'd ever run into a cheerleader. The French writer never got a chance, dying a few decades before the wholly American creation of suited-up, screaming sideline supporters appeared.

Organized cheering for sports teams began in the Ivy League in the 1880s with all-male "pep clubs" leading supporters in cheers. The practice spread, but actual cheerleading didn't commence until the late 1890s, when guys moved out from the stands where the pep leaders hung out and stood near the field in an attempt to cajole fellow fans to go wild for their team. Jack "Johnny" Campbell at the University of Minnesota is recognized as the first to make this transition in 1898.

This type of support, and the corresponding word *cheerleader*, were also almost certainly developing around the same time back in the Ivy League. We know this because future U.S. President Franklin Delano Roosevelt wrote while at Harvard University in 1903 about being "one of the three cheer leaders in the Brown game." By the 1920s, *cheerleader* had become a generic term for a person showing support for any activity.

While football cheerleaders today are primarily athletic women, females weren't regularly invited to participate until the 1940s and men now make up only about 10 percent of cheerleaders worldwide.

END RUN

In our prevailing high-flying version of football, the *end run* or *end around* isn't too sexy. But there was a time when these sweeping sprints toward the outside of the line of scrimmage were pretty gutsy. With less blocking power in these outside sprints, these plays were such a gamble that one of the sport's first great coaches, Amos Alonzo Stagg, wrote in his grandiosely

Leadership language

Chain of command is a big part of the football jargon. There are *field generals* and *team captains* whose scope of responsibility extends well beyond blocking, tackling, or throwing and running the ball. Those terms were unmistakably borrowed from the military world, but some may not be aware that two other well-known bits of leadership language—*coach* and *quarterback*—are also hand-me-downs.

Coach (and *coaching*) were academic designations in England in the mid-1800s. Back then, a coach at a place like Oxford University was a private tutor (usage that came from the idea that a student was helped along, as if in a coach, to success on a test). The terms crossed over into sports, particularly in rowing, by the final decades of that century. In the United States, baseball had already established the manager as the key off-the-field persona, but football adopted the coach designation early on.

The gridiron took the term *quarterback* from rugby. As is the case in football, rugby's quarterback was positioned just behind the forward line. Still, it's safe to say that football's application of the word—and the position's overall importance in that American usage—led to the use of *quarterback* to describe an important person in an array of instances by the 1930s.

titled 1893 book, *A Scientific and Practical Treatise on American Football,* that end runs should be used sparingly. "Long runs . . . cannot be expected, and the captain must be contented to work steadily up the field by short gains," he wrote with his coauthor Henry L. Williams. "After several dashes into the line, of this kind, an end run suddenly carried into execution may have considerable chance for success."

In an idiomatic sense, an *end run* came to describe an effort to sidestep an adversary or obstacle. It was popular among military leaders in World War II. In 1951, Winston Churchill brought up the expression when reminiscing about the invasion of Italy during that conflict. General Dwight Eisenhower planned to send a division away from the central fighting straight to Rome—something Churchill supported. "I had, of course," he said, "always been a partisan of the 'end run' as the Americans call it."

GAME PLAN

From college football's beginnings in the late nineteenth century, its developers sold the sport as a game requiring sophisticated strategies. Yet, strangely, the term football spawned to best reflect this approach—*game plan*—wasn't used until many decades after gridiron action got underway.

The delay may be due to the crazy con that student-athletes are just fun-loving amateurs. Early on, this deception wasn't so much about sheltering fans from the knowledge that players were getting fat envelopes full of cash after great performances; it was more about hiding how tactics were created. In the sport's formative years, many believed professional coaches undermined the purity of the game and should be limited in what they were allowed to do. In fact, remarkably, sideline coaching wasn't fully sanctioned in the college game until 1967.

Considering that context, avoiding phrases like *game plan* may have helped deemphasize the coach's role in college football's emerging days.

Still, even if there was an effort in some circles to minimize knowledge about the extent of coach involvement, journalists weren't fooled forever and, by the mid-twentieth century, reporters were regularly covering game plans in their football dispatches. (Geek note: The term *playbook* far predates its sports application, having been used in conjunction with dramatic plays as far back as the 1500s; still, the expression *taking a page out of another's playbook* is a late-twentieth-century creation, so it may very well be football-inspired.)

Outside of its use in football and other athletic endeavors, describing a strategy as a game plan gained traction in the 1960s. One regular practitioner of the expression was former U.S. President Richard Nixon, who was generally a sports metaphor enthusiast (see "Full-court press" on page 45). Unfortunately for him, most people found out about this proclivity while listening to the Watergate tapes.

A final point on game-plan complexity: The vast array of passing schemes and running options always on the menu allowed political advisers to steal *ground game*, an expression for a ball-carrying attack that has been a part of football since the 1920s. By the 1980s, the expression was used to describe a campaign's ability to mobilize supporters on the ground, so to speak, in order to get out a favorable vote.

HAIL MARY

Any good Catholic—or religiously curious person—knows a *Hail Mary* is a prayer sometimes offered as a penance and other times as a plea for a little divine intervention. While the church may have come up with the supplication, it's football that peppered it with dramatic panache, propelling the expression into a catchall for any long-shot effort.

Cut to December 28, 1975: The Dallas Cowboys were trailing the Minnesota Vikings in the NFC divisional playoffs with twenty-four seconds left in the contest. With his team at midfield, the Cowboys' longtime quarterback Roger Staubach knew he needed to take what was potentially his last crack at the end zone. Lacking many options, he called a simple play: throw the ball as far as he could in the direction of receiver Drew Pearson. Improbably, Pearson, after colliding with his defender (who helpfully fell to the ground), hauled in the pass for the game-winning touchdown.

"It was a play you hit one in a hundred times if you're lucky," Staubach said after the game. "I guess it's a Hail Mary pass. You throw it up and pray he catches it."

The metaphor was compelling, and a Hail Mary (football edition) was embraced throughout the sport—and beyond. During the 1982 trial of John Hinkley Jr., who had attempted to assassinate President Ronald Reagan, a television camera operator described an effort to lift his camera over a crowd in the hopes of getting some good footage as the event was unfolding. He riffed on Staubach's phrase, calling the maneuver "a Hail Mary shot," which we can only hope was an unintended pun.

HANDOFF

When it comes to the origin of idioms, basic sports jargon can sometimes hoodwink you. For instance, for most people, football's *fumble* looks like the source for non-sports-related mess-ups of the same name (example: "Darn, I fumbled that introduction"). But the term was used way back in the seventeenth century—well before players strapped on shoulder pads.

At first glance, a *handoff* might seem a similar situation, as the term also existed before football coaches were spouting about the play. But in this case, America's gridiron gave the term its current idiomatic meaning, which communicates any sort of handover.

At the beginning of the 1900s, British rugby players coined *handoff* to describe a player on offense pushing an opponent away while carrying the ball. (This is something similar to what we call a stiff arm nowadays.)

But when Americans modified the rugby rules for football, the term *handoff* didn't make the cut. In fact, it wasn't even originally used to articulate transferring the ball from quarterback to running back. The phrase finally entered the lexicon—at least for sports journalists—by the 1930s, and that usage led to a more general application by the 1950s, meaning to give someone something (either literally or figuratively).

HUDDLE

In the sixteenth century, *huddle* entered the English language to designate "a mass of things crowded together in hurried confusion." Less than a hundred years after that, its meaning evolved to describe "a confused crowd." This definition dominated for generations. (Think, "Give me your tired, your poor, your huddled masses yearning to breathe free" in Emma Lazarus's poem *The New Colossus*, which is etched into the base of the Statue of Liberty.)

The (nuclear) football

The most important football of them all—known by national security experts as the Football—isn't even a sporty projectile.

During the 1962 Cuban Missile Crisis, military top dogs decided U.S. President John F. Kennedy needed to be ready at any time to launch a nuclear strike. To make that possible, a black leather briefcase filled with key codes and communications equipment always traveled with the president in case he wanted to send missiles in the direction of a Cold War foe.

But why is this portable Armageddon starter kit, which is still used today, called "the Football"? Its formal title is the "president's emergency satchel," but it earned its colloquial name, according to former Secretary of Defense Robert S. McNamara, because an early code word for the United States' nuclear war plan was "Dropkick." The logic went that "Dropkick" needed "the Football" in order to get underway.

But football grabbed the word for a different purpose. In the nineteenth century, the game featured periodic "conferences" in the backfield between certain players. But it took a while for eleven offensive players to come together behind the line of scrimmage for a preplay chat. Depending on who you believe, between 1914 and 1921, either Bob Zuppke at the University of Illinois or George Foster Sanford at Rutgers University was the first to consistently huddle up his players. For what it's worth, Zuppke defended his innovator significance "with vigor," according to his biographer Maynard Brichford.

Though the established definition for *huddle* at the time didn't match this formation—the group gathered in a circle in part to avoid confusion in playmaking—newspapers had dubbed them *huddles* by 1921. (It's unclear whether the coaching trendsetters first used the title or followed the journalists.)

Regardless, many in the football establishment weren't initially sold on this formation. In 1924, the *New York Times* ran an article intimating the huddle would be outlawed imminently. (Concerns ranged from how it slowed down the game to how it created unfair motion just before the snap of the ball.) In 1927, an unnamed "famous" football coach was still grousing to a journalist that the huddle "gives too many cooks a chance to express an opinion, and some of them haven't any."

Undeterred, proponents ensured the huddle survived, and its imagery spawned a new popular meaning for *huddle*—a private or intimate confab—by 1929.

MONDAY MORNING QUARTERBACK

Conventional wisdom would suggest that *Monday morning quarterbacks*, the more after-the-fact relatives of "Armchair quarterbacks" (see page 56), were created with the National Football League in mind. After all, pro football is a favorite Sunday activity for millions of Americans. So it seems to follow that the next day would be when you'd dissect—and criticize—the mistakes made by your favorite NFL club.

Despite that assumption, *Monday morning quarterback* was a college football creation and predates the ascent of the NFL. In 1931, the college game was still king and many pundits were criticizing it for becoming way too much of the focus on college campuses. That December, Harvard University's Barry Wood, who was the country's reigning all-American quarterback (as well as being a Phi Beta Kappa), gave a speech in defense of his game.

"The answer to overemphasis was to be found not on the field, but in the stands where sit what Wood called 'the Monday morning quarterbacks,'" the *New York Times* wrote after the speech.

It's not clear whether the erudite Wood, who would go on to be a successful doctor, coined the idiom, but it's the first known reference in print. Equally puzzling is why these post-game complainers didn't do their grousing on Sundays, as the college game was a Saturday event even back then. Okay, lots of folks would be going to church on Sundays, but wouldn't there be a little time for football contemplation? Perhaps Monday was the first opportunity to get back around the water cooler at the office and properly discuss. However it was spawned, almost immediately after Wood's usage, the term was embraced both in football and elsewhere to mean second-guessers.

PUNT

Punt has meant many things in the English language: It's the word for a shallow flat-hulled boat good for going down a stream. *Punter* has been slang for *gambler* since the early eighteenth century. And, as anyone who's watched a little football on a Sunday afternoon knows, it's a form of kicking that involves booting the ball before getting crushed by oncoming defenders.

The latter formulation, which is where we get the figurative use of backing out or giving up, was truly an accident. Most linguists believe that *punt* in the kicking sense was a mispronunciation of the older word *bunt*. To bunt meant—and still means in baseball—to strike or push. When rugby began using it around 1845, the *B* had magically become a *P*.

Americans co-opted the misspoken word, and punting became a part of football. In the beginning, the sport had various types of punts. There was a *punt-out* and a *punt-on*, as well as the garden-variety punt. The surviving fourth-down staple is what inspired people to throw their hands up and say, "I'm punting" when they couldn't solve a problem. It was used regularly in conversation by the mid-1960s.

RUN INTERFERENCE

Running interference is a dangerous business. No, not helping out your buddy who is in trouble with your sour boss, but performing the original meaning of the phrase. Back in the late nineteenth century, to *run interference* meant one thing: to perilously align blockers in front of a ball carrier and knock everyone out of the way on his behalf.

Unexpected term from football: Ivy League

Forget esteemed faculty or Nobel Prize–winning alumni, the Ivy League was created for one purpose—sports. And, although the founding schools competed in pursuits such as baseball, basketball, and track and field, there is little doubt the conference was devised with football in mind.

It may be difficult to believe now, but the eight universities that came together to form the Ivy League—Brown, Columbia, Cornell, Dartmouth, Harvard, Pennsylvania, Princeton, and Yale—were the powerhouses of Eastern football in the first half of the twentieth century. At least one reporter went so far as to dub them the "Big Eight" because of their prowess on the gridiron.

The flora-inspired name was allegedly the doing of Stanley Woodward, a reporter for the *New York Herald Tribune*. On October 14, 1933, he wrote about "our eastern ivy colleges," referring broadly to these institutions. A direct reference to the *Ivy League* arrived in an Associated Press article written by Alan Gould in 1935. No one was ever explicit about it, but it's safe to assume the green vines growing on these august schools' walls led to the designation. Despite being regularly dubbed the Ivy League by journalists throughout the 1930s, these eight universities didn't formally become a football conference until 1945.

Football's decision to allow this tactic was a complete game changer. Indeed, it was a key component in distinguishing football from rugby, which prohibited running out in front of the ball to prevent tackling. After interference was sanctioned in 1889, a formation known as the flying wedge was created. This wall of human obstruction was stolen from an even more serious group—the military. Basically, a phalanx of players would run in front of the one with the ball, picking off any poor defender who thought he could break through the wedge. It was effective for scoring and, tragically, a killer.

The total number of casualties during this period isn't clear, but a 1905 *Chicago Tribune* article claimed there were eighteen college fatalities in that season alone. If so, there's a very good chance running interference played a big role in many of the deaths. The wedge's lethal nature was so bad that U.S. President Teddy Roosevelt stepped in and required a summit that year at the White House with the sport's top coaches of the time. The upshot was a limitation on the most egregious forms of interference.

Over time, *interference* became a pejorative on the gridiron. As a result, the act of *running interference* received a marketing makeover, getting a name-change to *blocking*. In the game we now watch, *interference* is primarily mentioned when a player acts inappropriately on a thrown ball, creating pass interference. But in the late 1920s, when blocking was still known as *running interference*, writers were inspired by the hard work of offensive linemen on behalf of a ball carrier and used the term idiomatically to represent providing assistance.

RUN WITH THE BALL

Run with the ball is a phrase that may have many sporting parents. (Just think of the games where running with a sphere is required and you have a contender.) Even so, the *Oxford English Dictionary* indicates the phrase (along with the similar *carry the ball*) got its start in North America, and since none of the continent's other major ball sports rely on running with the ball the way football does, we'll mark this one down for the gridiron.

If that's the case, football can thank its sister game of rugby. Though it is likely a myth, a student at England's Rugby School is often credited with the idea of running with the ball. The story goes that in the 1820s, William Ellis Webb was playing a game of soccer when he was somehow inspired to pick up the orb and start sprinting with it. From there, the game of rugby—named after his school—was born.

Whether or not it's true, running with the ball was a central part of football from the very start. It wasn't until around 1924, when major changes were made to the shape of the football, that the game really embraced throwing rather than almost exclusively running. The descriptive nature of the expression meant that it was showing up in print in game stories way back in the 1880s. By the 1920s, it had gone metaphorical to mean taking responsibility for an act or situation.

TIME-OUT

As any three-year-old can tell you, a *time-out* can be very contentious. It was no different in sports when the time-out stoppage was conceived. The football term was in print by 1896 thanks to Walter Camp and Lorin F. Deland, two of the sport's great developers. The pair defined it plainly in their book *Football* as "Time taken out by the referee when play is not actually in progress."

This vague explanation reflected football's underlying purpose as a gentlemen's game (albeit a violent one). Though time-outs were allowed, they weren't governed by structured rules. Instead, team captains were just asked in the name of sportsmanship to keep them to a minimum for substitutions or injuries and to try to limit each one to a maximum of two minutes.

Bad call: The competitive nature of such an intense pastime got the better of most team leaders, and abusing the time-out to gain an advantage ran rampant. It got so appalling that in 1906, as part of a major overhaul of the rules, football's governing body limited teams to three time-outs per half without a penalty. Unfortunately, stalling via the time-out continued over the next few decades—so much so that a former Yale University star argued in a 1927 *New York Times* article that the break should be scrapped altogether. (He failed, but the rule has been tweaked over the years.)

With basketball also using *time-outs*, the term became ubiquitous in American culture. By the 1930s, people were asking for time-outs from their busy schedule. In the 1950s, the dreaded time-out for children entered the conversation, and in the 1970s, the computer world adopted the phrase to describe an operation stoppage.

Chapter 4

HOCKEY

**"There's no power play taking
place in Washington."**

—Secretary of Defense Donald Rumsfeld dismissing allegations
in 2006 that there were tensions over the Pentagon's
growing influence in intelligence gathering

Fans of this useful term should give a respectful tip o' the mask to both the game of hockey's most important ancestor and the incomparable Bard of Avon. *Bandy* was the name of hockey's key precursor, and William Shakespeare was the man who brought the word to the mainstream.

The sport of bandy dates back to at least the sixteenth century, and its rules could vary based on where you lived in Europe (sometimes there were goals and other times there might be holes—golf style—in which to deposit the ball). Still, generally speaking, the game was played with a curved stick, and it proved a central first step in the eventual development of ice hockey.

Bandy still exists as a niche game played on ice in countries like Russia and Sweden, but back in the day, it was a pretty happening sport. It was so renowned that none other than Shakespeare made note that "bandying" was outlawed on the streets of Verona during a rare moment of less-than-heartbreaking drama in *Romeo and Juliet*.

It's Shakespeare who helped popularize the figurative meaning of trading words (or looks) as quickly as passing a bandy ball. In *King Lear* and *Taming of the Shrew*, for example, he employed the phrases *to bandy hasty words* and *to bandy words*, respectively.

FACE-OFF

There's no denying that the 1997 film *Face/Off* gave this phrase a creepy idiomatic turn. (If you've never seen the Nicolas Cage–John Travolta face-swapping action thriller, no reason to put it on your must-see list.) But long before the two stars were trading faces on the big screen, *face-off* got its start in sports.

No doubt, average sports fans would—and should to some degree—assume the eye-to-eye puck drop in hockey served as the term's genesis. That said, hockey didn't immediately embrace the phrase. When some students at Montreal's McGill University memorialized the game's first rules in 1877, *face-off* wasn't included as part of the lingo. Instead, the writers called the puck drop a *bully*, which is the same term used by field hockey (it's also sometimes called a *bully-off*.) We know that by 1897, when an exhibition hockey game took place in New York, *face-off* had become the term of choice.

With hockey's early uncertainty, lacrosse fans can also stake some claim to this phrase. Like hockey, lacrosse didn't exactly use *face-off* initially—though the sport's innovators did come a bit closer. When the first comprehensive book on lacrosse came out in 1869, it referred somewhat ambiguously to what's now called a face-off. It was, the author W. George Beers wrote, the moment when opposing players "faced" for the ball. By 1889, the rules for lacrosse games had made the switch to *face-off*.

Whether lacrosse or ice hockey got to face-off first, the faster growing ice hockey tied the term to frozen surfaces everywhere. Interestingly, both hockey's McGill rules and Beers's book were written in Montreal, so some cross-pollination is likely. By the 1920s, language embraced *face-off* to mean showdowns of all types.

Asking about the origin of *hat trick* would be a great grand finale question on a U.S. or Canadian game show. The knee-jerk North American answer would be to say it's an ice hockey term, but the reality is it's a cricket creation.

A brief game changer: Other skating sports

Even if you take away the helmets, gloves, pads, pucks, jock straps, and sticks, the final key piece of equipment in hockey—the skates—are a fountainhead for language. In particular, *skating circles around someone, skating on thin ice,* and maintaining the *inside edge* are all useful to have in your everyday arsenal.

The concept of thoroughly outclassing somebody by skating circles around them was already in print by the first decade of the twentieth century. And it could be a lot older. The first book on figure skating, which talked about making circles (what other figure would you start with?), dates back to the eighteenth century. So, practically speaking, good skaters had been literally skating circles around—or at least better circles than—their opponents for quite a long time. It's also possible that it sprang from the similar but more widely used metaphor *running circles around someone,* which emerged in the late nineteenth century.

The hat trick tradition (and the phrase) first took hold at an 1858 cricket match in Sheffield, England, according to the Association of Cricket Statisticians and Historians. One of the great bowlers of the time, H. H. Stephenson, performed a tremendous rarity—hitting three straight wickets in three

Having the *inside edge* also has a bit of a murky past. It could have been inspired by anything from mountain climbing to getting the best location when sitting down at a table. But the *Oxford English Dictionary* credits the inner part of a skate as the source for this phrase that means "having the advantage."

Skating on thin ice is a bit easier to pinpoint. Multiple sources say the phrase that means "being in a precarious situation" earned its stripes as a metaphor in 1841. Ralph Waldo Emerson coined it in his essay "Prudence": "In skating over thin ice," he wrote, "our safety is in our speed."

Beyond those idioms, *skate* is also slang for departing quickly ("Let's skate from this lame party") or for getting away with something or sliding by ("I just skated by on that test").

For those wondering, *cheapskate* doesn't come from the ice. It's a play on another meaning for *skate*: a nasty or despicable individual.

straight throws (for those not cricket-inclined, this occurrence is nearly as uncommon as a no-hitter in baseball).

Impressed with the feat, elated onlookers passed a hat around for spectators to contribute a little something extra for Stephenson. From there the story varies. Some say the proceeds were used to buy a hat for the man, while others believe Stephenson took the cash and bought a chapeau for himself. It's also possible he used the money for another purpose, and the hat being passed around led to the term. What we do know for sure is this event spawned the phrase *hat trick*.

While cricket started the term's usage, it's hard not to give hockey its due for nurturing it. Since at least the 1920s, it's been used to describe when a player nets three goals in a game. Fans love the concept so much, they still throw their own caps onto the ice in these moments (which happen far more often in hockey than in cricket). There are even variations: A *pure* or *natural hat trick* is the notching of three consecutive goals without anyone else scoring in between. A *Gordie Howe hat trick*, named after one of the sport's great, tough goal producers, is a cheeky reference to a player who scores a goal, provides an assist, and then gets into a fight.

Hat trick is used in numerous other sports to describe a "Trifecta" (which itself was originally a horse-racing term [see page 145] before also crossing over, in the 1970s, to represent three of something). For example, when a baseball hitter strikes out three times, it's called a *hat trick*. It was also applied to three-of-a-kinds in nonsports activities in the first decade of the twentieth century.

POWER PLAY

As you can see elsewhere in this section, ice hockey doesn't possess complete custody of many of its most cherished idioms. *Power play* is another of those split-home phrases. If you took a time machine back to the 1920s and wanted to discuss power plays with sports buffs, they'd start talking about football.

From the beginning of the twentieth century, the gridiron used *power play* to explain a running attack that featured a ball carrier barreling down the field under the heavy protection of his teammates. But it took on special meaning at the University of Southern California when Howard Jones led his Trojans to three Rose Bowl victories in four years from 1929 to 1932. During that stretch, sport columnists across the country were calling Jones's deeply fortified push-forward running scheme *the power play*.

Hockey writers picked up the phrase in the first few years of the 1930s. At first it didn't take on its modern meaning, which is a situation when one squad has more skaters on the ice than the other on account of a penalty. Back then, a power play was an even-sided strategy in which defensemen, who according to the tactics of the day normally stayed relatively close to their own goal (even as their forwards were attacking), would become part of the offensive effort. In 1933, when superstar Eddie Shore won the National Hockey League's most valuable player trophy, the *Canadian Press* wire service lauded the plucky defenseman for being the "dynamic mainspring of the Boston Bruins' 'power play.'"

The details of its linguistic transition are obscured by time, but by 1936, *power play* reached its current definition. (Prior to 1936, if a team had fewer players, it was simply called *shorthanded*.) While the term *power play* waned in importance in football with the increased use of passing, it became a staple of hockey language.

Power play began enjoying regular colloquial use in the 1940s as a general expression for a strategically manipulative maneuver from a point of strength. Because of the timing, it's not clear if the stimulus was football or hockey. Regardless, even if the gridiron started the trend, most folks (with the exception of you hardcore lacrosse, water polo, or one-day cricket players who use it as well) attach the phrase to the ice.

TONSIL HOCKEY

All right, we can be pretty sure that this hockey-inspired activity hasn't taken place during the heat of a game. Still, in honor of the sport, *tonsil hockey* speaks to the frenetic nature of the puck bouncing around an ice rink.

The euphemism for tongue-smacking kissing was a creation of the 1980s, showing up in slang compilations in 1986. Arguably, it goes down—with big hair and Cabbage Patch Dolls—as one of the stranger creations of the decade.

To its credit, *tonsil hockey* has proved somewhat resilient. While use of the term isn't particularly trendy (other than in tabloid columns), it's certainly outlasted a similar term that appeared around the same time (*boxing tonsils*)—and big hair, for that matter.

Chapter 5

SOCCER

"I'm ordinary. I'm a soccer mom. I make sliced oranges and go and cheer [my kids] on."

—Former *Baywatch* star and *Playboy* playmate
Pamela Anderson

KICK OFF

Kick off is a nineteenth-century invention. First came the phrase, "I'm going to kick off my shoes" (Charles Dickens offered up that formulation to his readers), and then the sporting world used it to label a game's starting action. In the latter instance, the term came from Britain with soccer and rugby, which were, at the time, considered just different versions (or as the British put it, different "codes") of the same sport of football.

The first rules of soccer were devised in 1848 at Cambridge University. Yes, along with grappling with dead languages and advanced mathematics at this most hallowed institution, students also had time for games. Unfortunately, they didn't possess the sense to keep a copy of those original instructions, so the oldest version that currently exists dates to 1863. That edition of the rules talks about how the "kick off shall be determined by tossing." Though it doesn't specify, we can only hope the tossing involved a coin or something similar. Around the same time, there were rugby references to kick offs as well, so it's not clear which came first. Not long after, American football also started featuring kick offs to start contests. By the early twentieth century, the kick-off mania spawned use of the term outside sports.

MOVING THE GOALPOSTS

This idiom, in my mind, conjures up a shadowy villain—with handlebar mustache—tiptoeing around fields moving soccer goals or football uprights just before the ball reaches its destination (à la Lucy pulling the football from Charlie Brown in the *Peanuts* comics).

Whether you see it that way or not, that sense—or lack thereof—of fair play is the essence of what *moving the goal posts* is all about. It represents an unscrupulous last-minute change of rules. Nonetheless, the earliest known person to take a crack at using the goal for an analogy in print didn't see it that way. In a 1958 essay, Marjorie Carpenter, who was an academic from Stephens College in Missouri, got sporty. "If we are going to stimulate students to make critical value judgments, we have to be realistic about the goals of the student and then try to move the goalpost," she wrote, suggesting that realigning the goalpost was a good way to stretch students' minds.

Clearly, the erudite Carpenter (who quoted Benjamin Disraeli, Adlai Stevenson, and the seventeenth-century English poet Francis Quarles in this piece) wasn't a sports groupie. Come on, who moves a single goalpost? So it was left to others to give this phrase its full meaning.

Who deserves the credit is contested. The British invented the term *goalposts*, using it first in a soccer environment by the 1840s. In a 1990 *New York Times* article, an editor from the *Times* of London claimed credit on behalf of his country for moving them (he said it started with the kids' habit of sneakily shifting makeshift goalposts in recreational games).

At the same time, American football has a plausible origin story, thanks to a long-simmering debate over moving goalposts on the gridiron. Varying factions argued they should either be at the back of the end zone (putting them out of the way of receivers) or farther up (to aid the kicking game). This clash was taking up column inches in newspapers back in the 1920s and wasn't solved on the professional front until 1974, when the National Football League permanently placed them at the back of the end zone. This certainly aligned well with the idiom's ascent. It started becoming popular in the 1970s.

POLITICAL FOOTBALL

Despite the fact that it was often kicked about in the House of Lords and through diplomatic channels, an important early version of the football (aka the soccer ball) never saw a field. That was the *political football*, and editorialists were invoking it by the 1820s. On May 22, 1826, Evans and Ruffy's *Farmers' Journal and Agricultural Advertiser* suggested that the House of Commons had become "a political football, to be kicked at every turn and by all parties."

The ease with which the phrase was used suggests it had been around for a while, but that 1826 date puts the political football into play decades before soccer or American football set down their first formal rules. As a result, when that farm journalist was picturing a sphere before writing, it didn't look anything like the soccer ball (or oblong football) we now know.

Handcrafted foot-smacking spheres date back to at least the sixteenth century, but they were much smaller than our contemporary balls. Typically made of leather and stuffed with either wool or hair, these orbs were usually the size of a grapefruit. While imprisoned at Stirling Castle in Scotland, Mary Queen of Scots wrote in 1568 about watching a kicking game she called "football" using this type of ball. Ultimately a pig's bladder, and then a rubber one, would give these balls spring, but it's unlikely they had as much back-and-forth bounce as the issues that have earned political football status.

Soccer phrases that haven't made it big in the United States

Having devised and disseminated soccer's first modern rules, England is the cradle of the present-day version of "the beautiful game." Notwithstanding that great success, the country's ability to get people—at least on the American side of the Atlantic—to embrace soccer idioms has been a mixed bag. Phrases that haven't enjoyed wide crossover appeal include *own goal* (a self-inflicted mistake or blunder); *early doors* (initially a theatrical term for right at or near the start, it's now normally tied to soccer by British commentators and, as a result, used broadly); *route one* (a soccer phrase for a direct form of attack, it's also found a place in corporate circles for fast-tracking a project); *back of the net* (a successful action); a *head-the-ball* (a fool); *that's a red card* (referring to the referee's card that's given out for an egregious foul, it's also used to signal inappropriate behavior elsewhere); and *to have the ball at one's foot* (a largely faded seventeenth-century idiom for being in control).

Adult Americans may still lag behind the rest of the planet in their appreciation for soccer, but that doesn't mean kids don't flock to this sport. Approximately three million children sign up to play annually via U.S. Youth Soccer, and it's the mothers of those cleat-wearing souls who were pinned with the politically charged term *soccer moms*.

In the 1970s, the phrase popped up sporadically in print as part of straightforward descriptions of women with children playing soccer. But in the 1980s, when the number of American kids who competed in the sport crossed the million-mark threshold, journalists began putting meat on what the title truly meant.

"With the fall soccer season in full swing, a soccer mom finds her car filled with black-and-white balls, [h]olding uniforms and . . . dog-eared team photograph forms," wrote Chicago suburbanite Julie Kendrick in a 1984 newspaper column.

A picture of these harried mothers from the middle-class outskirts of major cities was formed. But the full weight of the expression's meaning wasn't felt until more than a decade later. In 1995, Susan B. Casey brought the term into the jurisdiction of politics when she ran for municipal office in Denver with the slogan "A Soccer Mom for City Council." A year later, during the 1996 U.S. presidential election, the soccer mom notion skyrocketed. Analysts insisted these women were the key swing vote in the race between President Bill Clinton and Senator Bob Dole.

Ultimately, soccer moms weren't too pivotal in the election, as Clinton dominated, outgaining Dole at the polls by nearly 9 percentage points. Still, the term did have an impact on language, as numerous soccer mom–inspired variations, like *NASCAR dads* and *hockey moms*, have entered the political lexicon since.

Part II

INDIVIDUAL
SPORTS

Chapter 6

AUTO RACING

"Don't worry, temporary pit stop. Sometimes I can be a little too bull headed and stubborn."

—Comedian and rapper Nick Cannon after
being hospitalized in July 2015

Telling the difference between idioms that come from everyday driving versus the specialized domain of auto racing can be difficult. For instance, while *firing on all cylinders, where the rubber meets the road,* and being *in the fast lane* all give off a track vibe, none likely has race-car lineage. *Firing on all cylinders* appears in 1920s articles on general automobile maintenance; *where the rubber meets the road* was created by Madison Avenue admen for Firestone Tires commercials featuring mundane motor vehicles like fire trucks, flat beds, and station wagons; and the *fast lane* is what the British (and most Americans) call the passing lane on the highway.

Taking that into account, here's what we know about putting *the pedal to the metal*: The phrase emerged in the mid-1970s and was definitely used in a car-racing context. One 1975 news report recounted an epic NASCAR battle between Bobby Allison and Cale Yarborough. "As they entered the third turn," wrote the journalist, "Allison tried to move lower but couldn't make any ground as Yarborough put the pedal to the metal."

Within a year of that reference, there are numerous examples of the phrase's application both in general driving and metaphorically to mean *giving it all you've got*. With the mentions so close to each other chronologically, this one might be too close to call.

In my mind, the tiebreaker belongs to longtime *New York Times* word columnist William Safire. In a 2005 article, he didn't give any hard evidence but endorsed the idiom's car-racing pedigree. His logic: Racing cars don't have any rubber or mats on the floor, so when a pedal is flattened, it really does touch the metal. With the same imagery of the fully depressed accelerator, Safire also asserted that *flat out* was launched at the racetrack as well.

PIT STOP

If you parse the phrase *pit stop*, the palpable question becomes, Who would want to take a break in a hole in the ground? As odd as it sounds, actual chasms made by humans did produce this term.

When automobiles featuring internal combustion engines became accessible in the nineteenth century, a new job emerged— the car mechanic. These pragmatic repairers realized that crawling underneath the carriage of a gas-guzzling steel beast was a dodgy proposition. So, to perform repairs, they dug garage pits three feet down or deeper so they could comfortably do their work below cars.

Although the first races in the 1890s were on the open road, closed tracks quickly followed, giving developers the opportunity to design a location where these machines could be fixed on the fly. Like the garages that already existed, the areas, which were first built at the dawn of the twentieth century, were called *the pits*. References to *pit stops* as a description for the car-racing activity can be found by 1915.

It should be said that in many cases, early repair efforts could be somewhat disorganized. For example, at the dawn of stock-car racing in 1950, "pit stops were rather chaotic," NASCAR Hall of Fame historian Albert "Buz" McKim said. "It was pretty much done by neighbors of the driver or a team owner looking for a way to get into the race for free."

Pit stops ultimately morphed into finely tuned choreography that nowadays can have a race car refueled and with new tires (among other adjustments) in twelve seconds or less. To every parent's lament, pit stops on a roadtrip with the kids take a lot longer.

Motor racing snatched the phrase *pole position* from the horses. In the late 1800s, writers would talk about the pole position in horse racing the way we now talk about *the inside track* (see page 148). Officially, the pole position was the name for each of a series of markers every one-sixteenth of a mile down the course, according to *The Language of Sport* by Adrian Beard. So, when a horse got nearest to the railing (and those poles), it was in a preferable location.

Journalists brought the same connotation over to car races in the first decade of the twentieth century. By the 1920s, the phrase

Language legacy of the Indianapolis 500

Most racing devotees know the phrase *gentlemen, start your engines* got its entrée at the Indianapolis Motor Speedway. Though there's some disagreement over who thought it up, credit is widely given to Wilbur Shaw, the racing shrine's president from 1946–1954, for first popularizing it. Euphemistically, it's been used as a rallying cry both for randy men in the presence of attractive women, and applied broadly to men and women to pump up and motivate a group.

More unexpected is the general belief that this granddaddy of all American car races also hatched the phrase *on the bubble*. In fact, the term was being used in California in the late 1940s, though with a different meaning. Newspapers took on meaning for the best spot on the starting grid. Here's how: By and large, race courses back then would have a big pole at the starting/finish line. Unlike now, when a person waves the checkered flag at the end of a race, the pole was used to hoist that signal for the winner. Consequently, the person closest to that spot at the beginning got the pole position.

We know it's beneficial to start out in front (and people say the phrase for all sorts of instances when they have an advantageous situation), but does having the pole position mean you're going to win? If auto racing is our guide, the answer is,

in both Bakersfield and Hayward, California, used *on the bubble* in 1949 to describe somebody in the "Pole position" (see above). This usage didn't stick; instead, the phrase popped up in Indianapolis race descriptions by the 1960s and represented being on the cusp of either making it or failing to qualify for the event.

A 1961 Associated Press article explained the original motivation for the idiom: "A qualified car can be eliminated by a better subsequent performance," the journalist wrote. "In racing parlance, the qualified driver with the lowest speed is 'sitting on the bubble'—waiting for it to burst when somebody turns in a better ten-mile run." This works, as the expression *bursting your bubble* had been around since the nineteenth century and was well known throughout the United States.

it really depends. A 2013 Formula One study by Pinnacle Sports found that 49 percent of pole position starters won their race. While those are pretty good odds, the same can't be said for stock cars. A breakdown that same year of the past twenty-five winners of NASCAR's Daytona 500 showed that only two pole sitters won the race and the average finish was a middling fifteenth place.

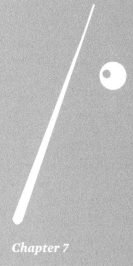

Chapter 7

BILLIARDS
(POOL)

**"I didn't have a problem with rejection, because
when you go into an audition, you're rejected
already. There are hundreds of other actors.
You're behind the eight ball when you go in there."**

—Actor Robert DeNiro on his early career

If you believe a billiards icon, the expression *behind the eight ball* had nothing to do with the game eight ball. It didn't even directly involve playing a game of pool.

Charles E. Peterson, the inaugural president of the Billiard Association of America and a fancy shot champion, credited a bank clerk named Allie Flint with concocting the phrase in a pool room in New York City sometime between 1914 and 1916.

Flint and his buddies enjoyed "Kelly Pool," a game in which each competitor blindly picks a small numbered ball for his eyes only. Balls on the table had to be pocketed in order, and the winner would be the first player to sink his corresponding full-sized ball. The thing is, as they got together during the lunch hour, the group didn't have a lot of time, and, in truth, they liked the gambling more than the pool playing. So after a while, they decided to cut out the middle activity (playing pool) and focus on the betting. To that end, they'd just pull the small balls out of a shaker bottle, and he who drew the lowest number won the wagered cash.

"Well, this Allie Flint was the original hard-luck kid," Peterson said in a syndicated 1941 column interview. "He was forever getting a big number. And it seems No. 9 fell his way more than any other. In a game of some 10 or 15 players a number that high was a bust-out. An eight might sometimes luck out—never a nine."

Hence, Flint lamented after continued losses, "There I am behind the eight ball again," according to Peterson. "It spread like wildfire all over New York and then over the country. It was the birth of the eight-ball blues."

The story has a mythical quality to it, and the idiom certainly has meaning in the game of eight ball (being behind that ball is a big strategic disadvantage). It's also important to note that this metaphor for being in a precarious situation became particularly widespread in the 1930s, after the game of eight ball had acquired a large following. Those facts do leave us a little behind the eight ball, so to speak, as to the phrase's origin.

DIRTY POOL

Anyone who's seen the 1961 classic film *The Hustler* with Jackie Gleason and Paul Newman needs no further evidence that pool can be dirty. (See the thumb-breaking scene for some graphic details.)

The word *pool* is interwoven with gambling. In the 1840s, the game's name referred to the pile of cash players threw in that would become spoils for the winner. Not unexpectedly, when money is at stake in an unregulated game, there will always be some cheating.

In the early twentieth century, for example, there were instances when grifters used loaded pool balls to achieve results. Or they played the "lemon game," a con for hustling an opponent into believing you are a terrible player before raising the bets and crushing the unsuspecting rube.

With so much scamming, it's mind-boggling that the phrase *dirty pool* didn't really emerge until the 1950s. The author Herman Wouk appears to have been out front when it came to using the saying in print, applying it as a metaphor in *The Caine Mutiny*. "I played pretty dirty pool, you know, in court," Lieutenant Barry Greenwald (played by Henry Fonda in the movie) says at one point in the book.

The phrase has faded a bit since its heyday in the second half of the twentieth century. But like the pool sharks who continue to scam, it's still very much a part of the action.

For you occasional pool players, here's a heads-up: a *lucky break* has nothing to do with that opening shot that knocks those nicely racked balls all over the table. That's the opening break. Originally, a *lucky break* represented a fortuitous run of point-scoring shots. And in billiards' developing days, luck had a lot to do with it.

Early balls were made of wood, but, in the seventeenth century, ivory became the material of choice. Not only was there a moral problem with ivory (at one point as many as ten thousand elephants were being slaughtered each year for their tusks), but there was also a playability issue. Changes in temperatures on a table could quickly warp balls. And with no central heating, this was a regular occurrence. The well-heeled, which included Queen Victoria, were so concerned about this that they actually heated their bumpers to try to protect against ruined balls.

The upshot is that these spheres often played in unpredictable ways, leaving much of the result to fortune. So using the word *lucky* to describe an accidentally successful series of shots was very appropriate at the tables. Newspapers took to the phrase by at least the 1880s. One paper, the *Magnet* in London, put *lucky* in quotes when describing a *lucky break* in an 1886 article, so it may not have been universal as a written expression at that point. Even if so, it caught on quickly, appearing as a turn of phrase in an 1890 U.S. serialization of the British novelist Benjamin L. Farjeon's book *Basil and Annette*.

The timing was also definitely lucky for this idiom. If players had been a bit more patient, the phrase might never have taken root because plastic balls, which roll with more precision, began replacing ivory at the start of the 1900s.

As for a *good break* or a *bad break*, both may have come from pool halls as well, but some word experts believe they started elsewhere. One fun (albeit iffy) theory has it that long ago, when a person was in legal trouble, the funds friends and family would raise to pay attorney's fees were called *breaks*. Perhaps the difference between *good* and *bad breaks* represented having enough money to cover those costs.

MISCUE

Miscue is an example of how words evolve over time. In 1838, the term for a botched cue shot was *miss-queue*. By 1869, it had transformed into a *miss cue* or *miss-cue*. It eased into its current form in the final couple decades of the nineteenth century. (That said, some were still writing *mis-cue* at the start of the 1900s.) There are some dictionaries that say this term comes from the theater where it means a slip of the tongue when *cued* to speak. But the common use of *miscue* to represent an everyday gaffe or flub became particularly popular in the final few decades of the 1800s at a time when it could be regularly read in newspaper reports on billiards—and was rarely, if ever, seen in papers for its theater purpose. This gives the pool hall the leg up over the stage as the place that, at the least, popularized the idiomatic use.

Now, this isn't a self-help book, but in case you're wondering, here are some tips for avoiding this calamity at the tables: Keep your cue level; make sure it's properly chalked; and be extra careful when you're aiming off-center in an attempt to put some serious spin on the ball.

And, if none of that helps, take solace in the fact that even the greats sometimes miscue—with a lot more at risk. In 1859, Michael Phelan and John Seereiter were competing in one of America's first high-profile, huge-stakes pool games. The prize was at least $15,000 (with side bets, the total amount is unclear; but we do know it was a tidy sum for the time). The winner would also gain the unofficial title of America's best pool player. Nine and a half hours into the match, Seereiter looked poised to win but reportedly miscued, opening the door for Phelan, who pocketed the necessary balls and a big wad of cash.

RUNNING THE TABLE

There is a lot we don't know about *running the table*. From a pool-playing standpoint, the strategy for clearing all your balls into pockets (aka running the table) varies greatly depending on who's talking. One guidebook insists that thinking three moves ahead is key, while an online expert uses a card analogy (kings, queens, jokers, and aces) to identify the best way to set up balls for the run.

From a language perspective, matters aren't much clearer. Making "runs" of balls—that is, consecutively dropping them into pockets—was part of the jargon of billiards in the late nineteenth century (the phraseology was used a number of times in an 1896 book called *Billiards*). But exactly when we brought the table into this particular conversation is fuzzy.

The famed *New York Times* word columnist William Safire tackled the topic in a 2001 article. He pointed out that the metaphorical use of the phrase to represent a clean sweep had become popular over recent years, and he quoted an expert who claimed the term, at the time, was about forty years old. But

Unexpected word from billiards: Fluke

The word *fluke* has a few meanings. It can refer to a type of flatfish, also called a summer flounder. It's been used to describe part of a ship's anchor as well. But we use the word most often to describe a stroke of unforeseen good fortune.

This last meaning evolved in the mid-1800s from trying experiences at the billiards table. Before technology made pool a more precise game, it was a contest of skill that also required quite a bit of luck, thanks in large part to ivory billiard balls that would regularly warp and, consequently, move imperfectly (see "Lucky break" on page 98).

Naturally, players needed a shorthand word to explain a poorly played shot that benefited from the shortcomings of the equipment. While *fluke* in the fish sense appears to come from Old Norse and the nautical definition of the word is likely Germanic in origin, the use of *fluke* in the popular sense in all probability comes from Old English. *Fluke* in that dialect meant *guess*, and it's easy to see that meaning mutating into a positive yet unplanned shot.

By the end of the 1880s, the word had broken out of billiards to mean any unexpected bit of chance. Some even used it as a synonym for a surprise breeze—though that meaning didn't linger for long.

Safire would later receive a letter from a reader who assured the journalist it was being bandied about by 1950.

All I can add is that in 1943, a journalist in New Castle, Pennsylvania, used it (at least conceptually). A reporter reminisced about the good old days when there were local pool players who could "break them and run 'em off the table."

For all that's cloudy with the history of this phrase, there's little doubt who did it best. In a 1954 exhibition, Willie Mosconi set a record, sinking 526 straight balls. Now, that's running a lot of tables.

Chapter 8

BOWLING

"I'm sellin' dope in each and every record store. I'm the kingpin when the wax spins."

—Rapper Ice-T from his 1988 song "I'm Your Pusher"

Bias may be the result of an accident. Well, at least the word might be (there is no excuse for pundits on the twenty-four-hour news networks).

One of the great legends of lawn bowling involves the Duke of Suffolk in 1522. He was partaking in a ball-rolling game when his sphere split. Needing a new orb, he went into his manor looking for an alternative. The best he could find was a round ornament on a banister. Figuring it was better than nothing, he had it cut off. The ball, which wasn't perfectly round owing to the sawed portion, rolled at an angle and, thus, lawn bowling's unique form of ball was born.

The story seems too fanciful to be true, but if it is, it was the uneven weight of that impromptu ball that produced the term *bias*. It was taken from an Old French term *biais*, which means a *slope* or a *slant*. Some support for the yarn comes from the timing: the word first entered English in this bowling sense in the early sixteenth century, around the time that the Duke supposedly crafted his makeshift ball.

The reason the word *bias* doesn't typically conjure up thoughts of sports is that it's been a general term meaning "being strongly inclined in one direction" since the seventeenth century.

KINGPIN

When you look at a set of bowling pins, they all seem the same. In ten-pin bowling, each one is fifteen inches tall and typically weighs three pounds, six ounces (though that standardized weight does vary). Other ball-rolling variations like duckpin or candlepin bowling aim at uniform pins as well.

So how did we get the regal term *kingpin* from this sport?

The truth is the word doesn't come from any form of bowling as we know it. People have been tossing things at arranged pins for at least five thousand years, when the Egyptians were playing the game (much to my disappointment, no ancient bowling shirts have been excavated . . . yet). Still, balls haven't always been the projectiles of choice.

One variation of this sport was kayle, which existed at the start of the nineteenth century. Rather than going with a roll, kayle players threw a stick (or bone) at a series of pins placed in a straight line. The game may have faded into total obscurity if not for the fact that the targets were pins of different sizes. And, you guessed it, the tallest and most centrally located one was dubbed the kingpin.

The kayle-inspired term was in print in 1801, and the waxed-lane version of bowling eventually adopted it. Nevertheless, in modern bowling, there has been some disagreement over which pin should be crowned. Most sources decree the number five, which is right in the middle of the other pins, the kingpin, while some rebels look to coronate the front pin (the number one).

When it comes to the word's metaphorical use, a super-important person on a team or in an organization could earn kingpin status by 1867.

Unexpected phrase from bowling: There's the rub

If this phrase, which means an obstacle or difficult situation, sounds familiar, it's because it comes from William Shakespeare's famed "To be or not to be" soliloquy in *Hamlet*. ("To die—to sleep. To sleep! perchance to dream; ay, there's the rub.")

But what exactly is a rub? No, it isn't something for basting meat. Shakespeare actually borrowed it from lawn bowling. While most lords of great British manors had gardeners to make sure their bowling greens were baby smooth, the wear and tear could lead to some bumps or nicks. These issues with the surface could impede the movement of the bowl and were known as *rubs*.

This bowling nuisance clearly intrigued Shakespeare as, even before *Hamlet*, the author made use of rubs metaphorically in *Richard II* ("'Twill make me think the world is full of rubs").

Chapter 9

BOXING

**"I'd like to throw my hat in the ring.
Now FIGHT, hats! Fight!"**

—Talk show host Conan O'Brien in a 2015 tweet

When boxing outlawed hitting *below the belt* (also known as a *low blow*), you'd think it was the dividing line, so to speak, between the sport's hella-violent past and its present as a tough but relatively survivable endeavor.

Think again.

The journey toward protecting the nether regions started with Jack Broughton, who put together boxing's original set of prizefighting rules in 1743. Broughton, a successful pugilist, devised his code after killing a man in the ring. Clearly, he understood the sport's most dangerous aspects and decreed the lower body was off-limits . . . well, sort of. Punching down south was apparently still okay, but boxers were prohibited from seizing an opponent below the waistline. He also abolished another act that appears to be an idiomatic inspiration—*hitting a guy when he's down.*

While Broughton improved things, he left many tactics legal that we'd call cheap, like some wrestling moves. In spite of his rules, deaths continued in the ring—most notably, a high-profile fighter named "Brighton" Bill Phelps. So in 1838, a revised set of regulations called the "London Prize Ring Rules" became the law. Loaded with detail, this new document explicitly prohibited blows below the waistband.

Even with that protection, these bare-knuckle struggles remained a blood sport. It wasn't until 1865 that boxing really entered the modern age with the Marquis of Queensbury rules. (Geek note: The Marquis, most believe, didn't write this document; he just lent his stature to it. Credit is due to his friend John Graham Chambers.) While ending below-the-belt attacks was nice, this code held the real key to making boxing less extreme—the introduction of gloves in prizefights.

Once swinging downtown was banned, referees began reminding fighters not to hit below the belt, giving the terrible tactic more publicity. By the 1870s, the phrase had become a description for an underhanded deed or cruel criticism. *Low blow* emerged as an idiom around the same time.

BLOW-BY-BLOW

While it didn't originate in the ring, *blow-by-blow* was boxing's early form of sports marketing. The word *blow*, as in a good smack, came from Scotland and Northern England in the fifteenth century. The catchy construction of blow-by-blow showed up in poetry before becoming a centerpiece of fight language. Sir Walter Scott famously wrote in his classic 1815 poem *Lord of the Isles*, "Unflinching foot 'gainst foot was set, Unceasing blow by blow was met."

Newspapermen stole the phrase to describe their comprehensive boxing coverage at the dawn of the twentieth century. For example, in August 1900, a New Jersey paper alerted readers that a bout would be "announced round by round and blow by blow." Over the next couple of decades, the phrase became the bedrock of many publications' hard sell. In July 1910, the *Post-Standard* in Syracuse, New York, bragged that famed boxing writer W. W. Naughton was onboard to explain "blow by blow in detail" the results of the Jack Johnson–James J. Jeffries title fight. In July 1919, an Ohio newspaper hyped its upcoming coverage of the Jack Dempsey–Jess Willard championship with a front-page headline, "The Story Blow-by-Blow."

As much as newspapers used the phrase, radio broadcasts in the 1920s really increased its exposure. Broadcasters would proudly point out they were providing real-time blow-by-blow accounts of fights. With the sports pages—and the airwaves—chock-full of the phrase, editors covering the news took notice. In the 1920s and 1930s, papers talked about blow-by-blow descriptions for everything from domestic disputes to election campaigns.

DOWN FOR THE COUNT

Time is a profound concept. A quick surf on the Internet will yield more philosophical statements than you should ever need on the topic. You've got Benjamin Franklin, William Shakespeare, Nelson Mandela, Sophocles, and Johnny Cash (need I go on?) all contemplating the wonder that is time.

Boxing's contribution to that conversation is the *count*. While rounds are timed (see "Go a few rounds" on page 113), it's those ten seconds given to a downed fighter that can be the difference between glory and ignominy. But if you want to get really deep about this battle with the clock, it wasn't always of the essence. In the sport's early days there was no count. Instead, fighters would scrap until one quit or couldn't get up off the floor. And it's that image that some experts believe gave us the idiom *down and out*—and the variation *down, but not out*. There isn't irrefutable proof, but a connection between boxing and this metaphor for tough luck, which was in print by the 1880s, looks likely.

What we do know about being down is that fighters once got more time than they do today. In 1743, the first formal rules gave a boxer thirty whole seconds to get up. It would be more than a hundred years before it dropped to ten.

This race against the clock enchanted wordsmiths. The proof: You can be *down for the count, out for the count, take the full count,* or *take the long count,* depending on how you handle your referee-appointed time. (Whether similar phrases like *don't count me out* come from fighting, gambling, or elsewhere is open to debate.)

While the world's obsession with time is, well, timeless, boxing's linguistic offerings to the discussion are relatively new. *Down for the count* didn't become popular until the first decade of the 1900s.

FLOORED

Boxing has a long history of inspiring English, but if there were ever a period when the sport deeply defined language—especially among the wealthy—it was Britain's Regency Era in the early nineteenth century. Known as the *fancy* back then, boxing was tremendously *en vogue* amongst the aristocracy (and the wannabe rich). So much so that a special slang dialect emerged as a way for hipsters who enjoyed the fights to communicate.

Many of these phrases didn't last. For example, these days you rarely, if ever, hear someone comment that a boxer *displays to advantage* when he's fighting well. You'd definitely get a quizzical look if you said *bellows to mend* to express a fighter being terribly winded.

Still, some terms did survive—and *floored* is one of them, along with *bruiser* and *daylights* (as in *knocking the daylights out of someone*), among a handful of others.

Floored was likely coined by the man who was the sport's first great beat reporter. Pierce Egan, a London-born son of Irish immigrants, had a gift for words and a deep devotion to pugilism. He was the first to call boxing "the sweet science"—and to make sure readers recognized his efforts at devising new phrases, he'd generally italicize them in print.

Case in point is *floored*, which he often slipped into his prose. For instance, in his story, "The Fancy on the Road to Moulsey Hurst," he discusses one fighter who has his heart "up to his mouth every moment for fear he should be *floored*" (Egan's italics). *Floored* also showed up multiple times in Egan's boxing opus *Boxiana*, which was first published in 1813.

Even if Egan wasn't the first, he surely popularized it. It caught on so quickly that contemporaries like Lord Byron (who was also a boxing fan) and, a little later, Charles Dickens both used the metaphor.

GLASS JAW

The chin isn't just a piece of anatomy in the boxing world, it's a state of mind. If you're tough, you can *take it on the chin*. If you're foolhardy, you're *leading with your chin*. And if you're an easy mark in the ring, you've got a *glass jaw*.

While the first two phrases emerged in the 1920s, it's the *glass jaw* that seems to have launched the metaphorical importance of the chin. As far back as 1891, baseball wags referred to a fragile pitcher as possessing a *glass arm*. Around the same time or shortly after, the *glass jaw* entered the fight game as a metaphor.

"The whole secret of the glass-jawed fighter is that he is born with a weak jaw," the *Indianapolis Sun* authoritatively proclaimed in 1904. "While many fighters can stand a lot of pounding on the vulnerable point, others will go out from the slightest jar."

This vivid picture of a handle-with-care chin charmed authors. Jack London, whose classics include *The Call of the Wild* and *White Fang*, referenced a boxer's glass jaw in his 1913 novel

The Valley of the Moon. Though it could have happened sooner, the term had clearly gone idiomatic by 1949, when a dictionary with the foreboding name *Criminal Slang: The Vernacular of the Underground Lingo* included *coward*, *weakling*, and *easy victim* in its list of *glass jaw* definitions.

But is a weak chin truly the boxing equivalent of that one spot on the Death Star where Luke Skywalker could defeat the Empire? Maybe not so much. It's just "a newspaper expression," Ray Arcel (who trained such greats as Roberto Duran and Larry Holmes) told *Popular Mechanics* in 1988. "We never used it."

GO A FEW ROUNDS

When the ancient Greeks first organized fights, they didn't need any rounds because fighters would beat the ever-loving stuffing out of each other until only one was left standing. More than a thousand years later, the British added a bit of decorum to the proceedings by creating breaks between timed slugfests. But even with that improvement, bouts either didn't mandate a prescribed number of rounds or set the limit inconceivably high.

Contemplate for a moment the 1889 prizefight between John L. Sullivan and Jake Kilrain. The bare-knuckle brawl lasted an astonishing seventy-five rounds. At the start of the twentieth century, a heavyweight championship match typically went a maximum of fifteen rounds—and currently, most boxing titles are waged over twelve rounds.

Use of *go a few rounds* (or *a couple of rounds*) to reflect an everyday confrontation took hold by the 1910s. Bearing in mind the length of early fights, nobody before then probably wanted to "go a few rounds"—even metaphorically—for fear that the altercation, verbal or otherwise, might never end.

In boxing's primordial times, *heavyweight* didn't really mean that much. You see, during the bare-knuckle beginnings of the sport, organizers hardly cared about being beefy. It really only mattered

Boxers that never do any fighting

There is no way that Jacob Golomb would have ever thought good, loose-fitting underwear would be his biggest contribution to society.

Golomb was a self-made man. An immigrant from Latvia, who had five dollars to his name when he turned twenty, Golomb would build the highly successful boxing equipment business Everlast Sporting Goods Manufacturing Co. When he died prematurely of a heart condition at fifty-eight in 1951, his *New York Times* obituary talked about how he developed the boxing gloves worn by every heavyweight champion since 1919. It also mentioned his philanthropic efforts, and how he'd been "on intimate terms with the sporting world greats," including Babe Ruth, Joe DiMaggio, Jack Dempsey, and Joe Louis.

But the tribute neglected to point out how, in 1925, he revolutionized boxing trunks by adding elastic around the waist. Before then, boxers used belts to keep up their shorts, and his innovation made the gear much more comfortable.

Golomb may have believed it was one of his minor achievements, but clothing manufacturers picked up on if you didn't have enough of it. The legitimate fear was that a scrawny puncher would die in the ring at the hands of a brawnier opponent.

From a verbal perspective, that meant that the word *lightweight* was a part of the pugilists' lexicon before *heavyweight*. A British

the change. Prior to that, men needed buttons to fasten their undershorts or used some other form of garment like a union suit, which was basically a one-piece long john sort of thing.

By 1930, elastic-waisted underwear, dubbed *boxer shorts*—or *boxers* for short—hit the market. They didn't necessarily catch on everywhere in the beginning but became vastly more common when they were issued to soldiers during World War II. (Geek note: John F. Kennedy's Navy-issued wartime boxers sold at auction in 2003 for $5,000.)

During the 1960s, boxers lost a lot of their allure for more form-fitting options, but they made a huge comeback in the mid-1980s as designers began rolling out quirky options like a pair from the company Joe Boxer featuring the iconic yellow smiley face.

This all culminated with the pop-culture tipping point in 1994 when U.S. President Bill Clinton was asked on MTV whether he wore boxers or briefs. His answer was "usually briefs," much to the irritation of Jacob Golomb fans everywhere.

slang dictionary from 1833 described a lightweight—one presumably too runty to battle a top fighter—at 154 pounds. While it further labeled someone under 126 pounds as a *little-one*, there was no mention of a heavyweight. (Idiomatically, *lightweight* became shorthand for an inconsequential person by the 1880s, while it appears *heavyweight* wasn't regularly entering conversation to describe an important individual until at least the start of the twentieth century.)

In fact, *heavyweight* was first used in conjunction with racehorses (those animals can be big). Still, the fight game used it informally by the 1860s, and amateur weight classes, which included heavyweights, were being mentioned in the following decade. (From a professional standpoint, eight categories, including heavyweight, were officially implemented in 1909.)

Despite not coining *heavyweight*, the boxing community gave the word the imagery it needed to become a useful tool. Unlike at the track, where the term rather blandly classified a horse by weight, *heavyweight* reflects true greatness in boxing. Famed boxing champion Rocky Marciano aptly riffed on what winning the belt at that classification means in popular culture: "What could be better," he said, "than walking down any street in any city and knowing you're the heavyweight champion of the world?"

IN YOUR CORNER

In boxing's early days, being *in someone's corner* really gave meaning to having a fighter's back. More than providing triage, strategy, and encouragement, these guys, who were dubbed "seconds," needed some of the same pugnacious qualities as their boxers.

From the beginning, prizefights were all about the profligate bets between the parties, and it was often the role of the seconds to settle up after these bouts. You can be sure the losing side wasn't too keen to part with their cash—so getting paid could be as contentious as the contest itself.

During the bout, seconds also had some hands-on responsibilities. Beyond occasionally pulling their guy to the side if he was knocked down, rowdier corner men looked to tip the scales by direct action. This was enough of a problem that the London Prize Ring Rules, which were first written in 1838, established the decorum for those in the corner. Not only were they not allowed to physically interfere during the fight, but they were also required to "refrain from all offensive and irritating expressions."

Along with setting regulations, the London Prize Ring Rules coined "the corners," describing them as "spaces to be enclosed by . . . marks sufficiently large for the reception of the seconds and bottle holders." Taking the phrase widely to mean "you're on somebody's side and willing to help" gained popularity in the middle of the twentieth century, as did telling adversaries to *go to your corners* when matters got too heated.

KNOCKOUT

To *knock*, as in *to hit* or *strike*, is an ancient word. Experts believe it dates back to before the 1300s and comes from the Old English *cnocian* or the West Saxon *cnucian* (please, don't ask for pronunciation guidance for either).

By the seventeenth century, it was being used in *knocked out* and *knocked down*. William Shakespeare used both: In *Henry the VI,* Part 1, he wrote, "Many haue their giddy braynes knockt out." And in *Henry VI*, Part II, he employed the phrase "knocke him downe."

Boxing took it in the late nineteenth century in the context of the *knockout blow*. This notion of a fighter flooring an opponent with one swing captivated people so much so that an 1890 issue of *Scientific American* devoted an article to explaining the mechanics of the devastating punch. The *knockout,* the product of the *knockout blow,* also entered the lexicon.

This infatuation with the power of the knockout blow appears to have served as the bridge to some of the idiomatic meanings we presently use. Calling someone a *knockout* for her impressive looks or using it to describe an elimination tournament took root in the 1890s—around the time the knockout in boxing was popular grist for conversation. And, we know a *knockout blow* itself came to mean a decisively damaging act of any kind.

ON THE ROPES

Muhammad Ali was more than one of the greatest boxers of all time—he was arguably the sport's most talented talker. The heavyweight champion was so poetically prolific that he merited a 2006 book called *Ali Rap: Muhammad Ali, the First Heavyweight Champion of Rap.*

With those dual talents, it makes sense that he was the fighter to revolutionize a way for dealing with being trapped *on the ropes*—long thought to be a dire predicament—and popularized a new idiom-worthy phrase for the strategy—the *rope-a-dope.*

Early on, peril on the ropes didn't exist because, quite frankly, there weren't any ropes. Fights were in open fields, and when permanent venues were created in the early eighteenth century, the combatants' platform didn't always have ropes either. Roped boundaries became a required part of the ring in 1838, but they were erected for fights prior to that date. For instance, boxing writer Pierce Egan wrote about Tom Cribb being "against the ropes" in his famed 1810 fight with Tom Molineaux.

That phrasing was modified slightly to *on the ropes* by the late 1820s. History has left hazy exactly when the phrase made its transition into a handy way to say someone was in a tough situation, but there are examples of that usage from at least the 1920s.

Whatever its beginnings, the idiom was in full swing in the mid-1970s when Ali created an antidote for the ropes-induced calamity. In his 1974 world championship heavyweight title bout against George Foreman, Ali gladly got stuck on the ring's borders. The untraditional ploy conserved his energy and, at the same time, tired Foreman, helping Ali to a knockout victory. The following year, the loquacious champion was calling the tactic a *rope-a-dope* (as in using the ropes to make your opponent act like a dope).

While it's possible somebody else in his camp thought up the phrase, Ali sent it around the globe. Not long after, others picked it up as a metaphor for creating vulnerability by wearing down an adversary or for befuddling an opponent by acting unconventionally—both of which could be used by anybody on the ropes in the real world.

RINGSIDE SEATS

You don't have to be a J. R. R. Tolkien expert to know that a ring is supposed to be circular. So when you see the likes of Jack Nicholson or Denzel Washington (or generations ago, Frank Sinatra and Joe DiMaggio) sitting in *ringside seats* around a square, it's absolutely worth a head scratch.

The phraseology is a relic of boxing's beginnings. The old-timey bare-knuckle fights didn't have the same level of production value found at modern matches. Fights were held in open areas, and a rudimentary circle, called a *ring*, was created to give the fighters a sense of boundaries (as was also the practice for other forms of one-on-one combat such as

Punchy language

Nothing is more central to the sport of boxing than the punch. Without that skill, you'll never win a fight. Yet, verbally, there was a time when it didn't, well, *pack any punch*.

During the first golden age of boxing in early nineteenth-century Great Britain, a *punch* in a boxing sense was marginalized language-wise. A number of dictionaries during this era had entries for the word, providing such definitions as "an instrument," "liquor," and "buffoon" (as well as the verb *to puncture*), but there was no mention of socking somebody in the kisser. Lest you think that *punch* (as in hitting) was merely slang that didn't rate for high-class reference books, the popular *A Classical Dictionary of the Vulgar Tongue*, which was published in several editions under a variety of names from the 1780s to at least the 1820s, also dodged it. Those volumes defined *punch* as "a liquor called by foreigners Contradiction" or "the name of the prince of puppets."

So where was the pugilistic meaning? It wasn't that it didn't exist at the time. It shows up in much of the period's boxing writing. But it wasn't the cool kids' first choice. To the wealthy elite who followed the sport and employed a special cockfighting). In truth, the outer edges weren't a major concern, because boxers of the time really were expected to just wail away at each other in the middle of the space rather than bob and weave.

boxing language (see "Floored" on page 111), *punch* didn't always make the cut. An 1821 article that ran in a number of British periodicals, including the *Edinburgh Journal*, dismissed the term's importance. "The old phrase of a punch to the g[u]ts is now termed an attack upon the *victualing office*," the writer explained.

Accordingly, *punch* had to wait until Americans embraced it in the first half of the twentieth century to begin totally pummeling the English language (although use of a *punching bag* as a person being figuratively beaten may have come about a bit earlier). Some of the first metaphors used were *beating somebody to the punch* for being first to something; *punch-drunk* for being dazed; and *punch line* for a joke's payoff (though some disagree about *punch line*'s boxing roots). Then came *roll with the punches* (for resilience), *don't pull any punches* (to act without limitation), *pulling punches* (being tentative), *sucker punch* (being duped), *punching above your weight* (competing beyond your normal level), *counterpunch* (to respond with force), *one-two punch* (a powerful combination of people or things), and *Sunday punch* (for a metaphorically powerful hit).

The decision to go oxymoron with a squared "ring" had taken place by the late 1830s with ropes marking off the area. Despite the geometrical shift, the language was set. The rules decreeing that boxers would compete in a square were maddeningly called the London Prize *Ring* Rules.

The primo position to be in, ringside seats have gotten a lot better over time. In 1719, one of London's first known boxing venues had the fighters brawling on a circular stage, measuring a roomy forty feet or so in diameter. Later configurations had the ring as a twenty- to twenty-four-foot square. Our modern-day bouts occur on platforms that are between sixteen and twenty feet, depending on the sanctioning body, thus giving front-row fans a far more intimate up-close-and-personal view.

The phrase *ringside seats* was in use by the 1860s, according to word maven Christine Ammer. And as shorthand for a fantastic position from which to scope out any sort of activity, the phrase was a go before the end of that century.

Despite the ring confusion, boxing linguists may have gotten it right with *square off*, though the connection to pugilism isn't 100 percent assured. If the term for a head-to-head confrontation, which could be found in print by the 1870s, did start with fighters, then at least they properly nailed the shape.

===== **SAVED BY THE BELL** =====

You can be *saved by the bell* at the end of a boring class and, if you're an early 1990s teen-television connoisseur, you can enjoy *Saved by the Bell*. But one thing you cannot do is be saved by the bell in a boxing ring.

It's true that under the sport's Queensberry rules, which were written in 1865 and widely accepted in their time, a boxer felled to the canvas could avoid a knockout and quite factually be saved by the bell if on the floor when a round ended. The reason: The referee wasn't allowed to continue counting a fighter out once the bell sounded. But that rule was gone from most codes by 1963, meaning the bell no longer had this protective quality.

From the language angle, by the time the rule changed, it was too late to—wait for it—unring that bell. In the 1890s, the concept of being *saved by the bell* was regularly being used in boxing match reports.

That said, if you're a regular user of the interwebs, one myth on this topic must be debunked. This phrase has nothing to do with a pervasive eighteenth- and nineteenth-century fear of being buried alive. During that era there were horror stories of people being incorrectly pronounced dead and then waking up six feet under . . . in caskets.

To prevent against such a calamity, some coffins were outfitted with bells that ran from the box to the surface. Conceptually, this allowed the recently not-so-departed to ring away when they awoke. While it's a fascinating historical footnote, there is no evidence whatsoever that anyone was actually ever saved by the bell in this situation or that the phrase was used in conjunction with this setup.

SECOND WIND

Before runners embraced *second wind* to indicate that life-affirming moment when you morph from agony to euphoria, the term belonged to boxers.

In the 1810s, newspapers were agog about how fighters who seemed on the verge of going down rebounded. They called it *second wind* and credited pugilists for the term's usage. An example: In an 1816 fight between Samuel Atkins and George Smart, London's *Morning Chronicle* wrote about the fifth round: "Smart had got, what boxers term, second wind."

For those insistent on the term's running roots, there is an early reference: an 1812 issue of the *St. James's Chronicle and London Evening Post* explained that a runner in a two-mile race "recovered second wind." But I'm duty bound to point out that the race featured a well-known boxer as a contestant, which likely led to inclusion of the phrase in that instance. (Why he was moonlighting in a running competition is unknown.)

Still, boxing's hegemony over the phrase didn't last long. Before the midpoint of the nineteenth century, *second wind* was being used in hard-core events such as hunting and climbing. (Geek note for you nautical buffs: *Wind* as a metaphor for breath dates back to at least the fourteenth century, so it's unlikely this phrase came from the sea.)

By the opening of the twentieth century, *second wind*'s connection to running was firmly established, but it was still used to describe bouncing back from fatigue in all sorts of physical activity. Metaphorically, it came to represent nonathletic forms of bouncing back by the 1870s. It has idiomatically stood the test of time. Just ask Billy Joel, who sang about it in the 1985 tune *You're Only Human (Second Wind)*.

SHADOW BOXING

In all possible senses, people have been fighting their shadows since at least classical times. The Greeks, for instance, had their own word for it: *skiamachia*, which translates into "shadow fighting" (or "shadow battle").

English embraced this idea as well. A 1748 article in London's *General Evening Post* told the story of one man asking another with some concern, "You [s]eem to be conjuring up a Shadow to fight with." References like this suggest *shadow fighting* began as more of a general linguistic device than merely a boxing term. It's not that fighters didn't do pantomime moves; it's just that there isn't much evidence they originally called it *shadow fighting*. In contrast, all sorts of important nineteenth-century writers used the term idiomatically. Among them were the poet Samuel Taylor Coleridge and the explorer Sir Walter Raleigh.

The sport may have been late to this fight, but by the 1870s, *shadow fighting* was definitely in the boxing realm. The transition to *shadow boxing* came at the start of the twentieth century. (It was in regular use by the time Ernest Hemingway inserted it into his 1929 classic *A Farewell to Arms*.) This ultimately gave us a good phrase for stalling on a straightforward or crucial action or for a supposed fight between two parties that doesn't yield any real results.

SPARRING PARTNER

You'd never tell a prizefighter's *sparring partner* that he is a wuss. Even under the guise of practice, it's a hazardous endeavor. To wit, the job was once rated the third-most dangerous gig in the world after high-wire walking and lion taming, according to Graeme Kent's *The Little Book of Boxing*.

Taking that into account, it's odd that journalists in the early nineteenth century mocked sparring. For instance, the leading boxing journalist of that era, Piece Egan, dismissed it as a "mock encounter." But keep in mind that, at the time, prizefighting was a bare-knuckle enterprise. That made sparring—an undertaking that included head gear and padded gloves—the legitimately weaker sauce. Still, that safety was also its attraction for the wealthy who enjoyed it, and rather than doing it for practice, these dandies competed in sparring as a pastime. Professional pugilism shifted to a gloved affair in the final decades of the 1800s, and around the same time the term took on its contemporary meaning as practice fighting.

The word itself—*spar*—got its start circa the 1400s as a verb signifying to strike or thrust. Its modern roots sprung in the seventeenth century when it was used as a noun for both boxing and cockfighting clashes held under special circumstances. Broadly speaking, the word had great appeal. Thomas Jefferson used it in 1825, writing, "These gentlemen had had some sparrings in debate before."

TAKE A DIVE

The formula is uncomplicated: almost any vintage film including mobsters and a forlorn boxer will feature one of the following phrases—*take a dive, tanking,* or *in the tank.*

Take a dive, as in purposely losing a fight, appears to have come first. Whether it was coined by organized criminals or someone like Damon Runyon, who knew how to put fictional words into the mouths of both boxers and underworld types, is unclear. We know it was in print by the 1910s and delivers the wonderfully straightforward imagery of a boxer making the choice to head directly for the canvas at just the right time. (Even if the concept seems Runyon-esque, I should note this type of conduct did occur. As the fighter and real-life basis for the movie *Raging Bull,* Jake LaMotta once famously quipped: "You win some, you throw some.")

Going *in the tank* was the allegorical end to the dive. In the nineteenth century, a *tank* was slang for a swimming pool. By the early twentieth century, if you took a dive in the ring, it made sense that you'd end up in the tank.

Both phrases have enjoyed idiomatic longevity for intentionally failing, but the tank has taken on wider meaning over the years. When a person *tanks* these days or the economy is *tanking*, it generically signifies failure. In other words, the fix isn't necessarily in.

THROW IN THE TOWEL

In boxing's formative years, nobody was *throwing in the towel* at a fight. It wasn't that pugilists weren't quitting, it's just that the towel wasn't the preferred symbol for "*Adios—I'm out of here.*" If they threw anything, it was the lowly sponge. Yep, that water-soaking inspiration for SpongeBob SquarePants was a staple at fights from the dawn of fisticuffs. (An excavated vase dated between 510 and 500 BCE depicts a bout and there is a boy watching while holding a sponge.)

In truth, it's unlikely either was tossed anywhere in the early days of fighting. But by 1860, dictionaries showcased *throwing in the sponge* to indicate both that a pugilist was done and, more broadly, as a metaphor for submitting. *Throwing in the towel* doesn't appear to have made its debut until the start of the 1900s.

As surprising as it might seem nowadays, *throwing in the sponge* was still being used in the second half of the twentieth century—although, by that point, the towel was the preferred symbol of defeat. The reason for the change may be that the towel definitely has more of that wave-the-white-flag ambience.

Throwing your hat in the ring provides some proof that boxing descended from Europe's early dueling rituals. Back in the 1500s, when somebody wanted satisfaction for a perceived slight, a little tangible drama was required to call out the offender. *Throwing down the gauntlet* was that bit of kabuki. (For those not schooled in the ways of this peculiar form of chivalry, a gauntlet was an armored glove.)

With armored gloves less common in the nineteenth century, a hat became the boxer's proxy. There is evidence of this practice from 1804, when a guy name Tim Belcher was itching to fight a brawler named Bill Ryan in London. "Belcher first threw his hat into the ring over the heads of the spectators, as an act of defiance to his antagonist," the *Morning Chronicle* recounted. Regrettably for Belcher, his confidence proved unfounded as he lost to Ryan.

The hat practice continued throughout the century, and there's a strong reason to believe that it gained prominence in the United States, thanks, in part, to America's early megastar, champion John L. Sullivan. Dubbed the "Boston Strong Boy," Sullivan continued the tradition of physically tossing a *chapeau* into the ring to indicate he was ready to brawl. Moving it into symbolic terms, Teddy Roosevelt, who was pretty tough himself, proclaimed, "My hat is in the ring" in February 1912 to indicate his decision to run for president that year.

Sullivan also had a lot to do with the popularity of another scrappy idiom: *take all comers*. In 1883, he went on a tour to fight anybody prepared to step into the ring with him. Sullivan and the media described this as *taking all comers*. While others had done similar stunts (and used comparable terminology), the fact that not a single man lasted four rounds with Sullivan captured the attention of the country on behalf of the expression.

The more generic the expression, the more difficult it is to pinpoint its beginnings. Ponder the all-encompassing *bring your A-game*. It may seem vague, but the rules of phrase origin are that the oldest reference gets to boast ownership. So until an earlier instance is found, golf carries the distinction here.

In the Summer 1969 issue of *Gentlemen's Quarterly*, the phrase made an appearance in a description of the Harbour Town Links in Hilton Head, South Carolina. "Harbour Town was not designed for Jack Nicklaus's game, since that would have made it impossible for the average golfer to negotiate, but it is golf at its challenging best," the journalist wrote. "In other words, bring your A-game, as they say."

Finding another contemporary mention proved elusive, making this usage fascinating. If only the *GQ* author had explained who the "they" were. There is one potential nonathletic explanation for the origin of this expression. According to distinguished word expert Eric Partridge, *A-game* showed up in 1949 to describe the highest stakes poker matches at a card room or casino. This could have served as inspiration. But even so, it was not a commonly used term at the time (and there was no sign "bring your" and "A-game" were used alongside each other).

Fast-forward to the 1980s, and the phrase began percolating in print again. Admittedly, there are stray baseball mentions in 1985 and 1986, but golf—and golfers—continued to be at the forefront of its use into the first half of the 1990s (after which it became widely used for "requiring your best"). At the Masters in 1987, for example, Curtis Strange succinctly concluded before the final eighteen holes, "You'd better bring your A game."

FOLLOW-THROUGH

Combining *follow* and *through* seems natural. But golf mavens deserve credit for smacking them together in a manner that expressed what it takes to finish just about anything.

In February 1891, a British publication called (I kid you not) *Golf: A Weekly Record of "Ye Royal and Auncient" Game* reflected the term's emerging popularity as shorthand for the final part of a swing. Ye *Record* decreed, "The club head should not be stopped abruptly, but should 'follow through,' as it is called—that is, the circle described by the club head should be continued till the whole force of the stroke is expended."

Soon, other 1890s golf guides began calling the technical skill "essential." (Cricket also adopted the expression around the same time and baseball followed suit a little later.) As for *follow-through* in one's daily life, its born-on date occurred by the mid-1920s. Nevertheless, it hasn't lost any of its importance in golf. Type "golf follow-through" into YouTube's search engine to access hundreds of videos trying to explain how to do it the right way.

GOLF CLAP

Respectful yet lacking exuberance, the *golf clap* has been a common act on the links since, well, probably the sport's inception. As a part of the English language, its history is shorter. The term began popping up in the 1980s and was used at around the same time as a sarcastic tool to represent being underwhelmed. While the 1990 movie *Men at Work*, starring brothers Emilio Estevez and Charlie Sheen as garbage men, wasn't a box office winner, it does deserve some applause for being at the forefront of referencing (and using) the *golf clap* to mock.

If you want to know how the clap is done, see the etiquette book *Golf for Weekend Warriors: A Guide to Everything from Bunkers to Birdies to Back Spasms*. It offers these instructions: "Simply cup your hands and let four fingers of one hand make contact, at the near molasses speed of a dangerous downhill putt, with the palm of the other hand. Clap quietly and never more than four or five times."

There are plenty of variations. Just check out any number of James Bond bad guys giving contemptuously down-tempo applause with what's known as the *villain clap*. There's also the *slow clap*, which is louder and more passionate than the golf version. If you want an example, stream the classic sports drama *Rudy*; a quality slow clap comes late in that film.

MULLIGAN

A request for a do-over after a bad golf shot is called a *mulligan*, but maybe it should be labeled an *Ike*. Why, you ask? Because while we're not 100 percent sure who the Mulligan in question was, we do know U.S. President Dwight D. Eisenhower was an early aficionado of the practice.

But before we get to Ike's story, who is the infamous Mr. Mulligan?

The most popular *mulligan* origin story takes place in the 1920s at the Country Club of Montreal. On today's streets, the St. Lambert–based club is located about thirteen minutes from downtown Montreal. But back then, it was a difficult journey.

Supposedly, hotelier David Mulligan and three playing partners took a car to the club one day, struggling over the uneven roads. Running late on account of the bumpy ride, the group rushed to the opening tee. Mulligan, who hit first, shot poorly. (Versions of this yarn blame Mulligan's flub on still being shaky from the drive.) He asked for a correction shot and received it. His partners then laid his name on any future requests for a replacement try.

Alternatively, there's John A. "Buddy" Mulligan, who worked at New Jersey's Essex Fells Country Club in the mid-1930s. This tale goes that Buddy was often challenged to stakes games by two members. He was disadvantaged in these matches as he came straight from work while his competitors had time to warm up. The lack of preparation often led Buddy to badly slice his first shot. Mulligan would then point to his lack of practice and ask for a replay. The members relented but named that practice after him. If this story is true, the expression moved quickly because it was in print in Texas by 1936.

Both stories lack definitive proof, but the United States Golf Association offers each up on its website, while suggesting that Buddy's anecdote may be the less credible of the pair.

What we do know is that beyond the rarefied country club realm, the man who deserves credit for bringing the mulligan to the attention of the masses is Eisenhower. As far back as 1947, the *New York Times* was writing about how Ike asked for mulligans after bad tee shots. Another article in 1955 reported President Eisenhower frequently used mulligans. Even into the early 1960s, there were stories about Eisenhower's affinity for the extra shot (along with an explanation of what a mulligan was), opening up *mulligan* for its metaphorical definition: getting a second chance.

Anybody who's ever played golf can quickly see the connection between *par for the course* and its idiomatic definition—typical or average for a situation. But the phrase makes even more sense if you know the origin of the word *par*. Its earliest English recording dates to 1601. The term was taken directly from Latin where it means "equal" or "equal in value." Initially, it was used in the phrase *par of exchange*, which meant setting the equal value of two countries' currencies in exchange (e.g., £1 is worth $1.60).

Before golf appropriated it, *par* was applied in other circumstances as well. In the eighteenth century, people would

Unexpected word from golf: Stymie

Doesn't it often seem that it's the little things in life that leave us *stymied*? If so, it's apropos, since a very small item—a golf ball—gave us the term's modern usage.

Stymie was a seventeenth-century Scottish word for a person who couldn't see well. This usage didn't have great staying power—though I don't know how saying, "You're such a stymie—you're trying to eat a boot instead of the haggis" wasn't a big hit.

In any event, duffers took it to the links by the 1830s to describe when a ball obstructs another ball on the green, leading to its figurative use in the twentieth century to mean being thwarted from doing something.

use *par* to discuss everything from their physical well-being to how economic markets were faring. Depending on the topic, *above par* could mean "in good health" or "overpriced." Similarly, *below par* could reflect "being under the weather" or "a discount." Phrases like *not up to par* and *on par* developed from these meanings. (That's why being *subpar* isn't good in the real world, but a godsend on the links, and vice versa with *above par*.)

In the nineteenth century, the word became a term for calculating golf strokes, and if you're looking for the exact answer to the question "What's par for the course?" it can vary, but as even a first-time golfer can tell you, most eighteen-hole facilities go with seventy-two strokes.

========================= **TEE UP** =========================

When a coworker kindly *tees up* a question at a meeting, that sweet soul is trying to make it easy for you to answer with eloquence and grace (whether you succeed is on you). The Scottish expression got its start in 1744 via golf's original code. The rule makers were so grateful for a little ball elevation on an opening shot that they referenced use of a tee in each of its first three rules.

As for where golf's fathers plucked the word *tee*, that's a bit of a mystery. Originally written *teaz*, it popped up in 1646—well before the game was formalized. Theories on its source range from a Gaelic word for house to a Dutch term that seems to describe the tee's shape.

Using *teeing up* to describe readying a ball for an opening shot was a known expression at the end of the nineteenth century. Its figurative use was in print by the 1930s.

Interestingly, a couple of other tee-related phrases almost certainly did not get their start on the links. The *Oxford English*

Dictionary posits that *teed off* is an offshoot of *peed off*, which is a shortening of *pissed off*. This has a logic to it, because while there are many bad golfers, it would take a supremely feeble duffer to tee off so poorly, so often, to spawn this idiom.

As for *suits you to a tee* (and variations, which sometimes replace *tee* with just the letter *T*), the little wooden golf peg doesn't appear to have any connection to "fitting you perfectly." More likely is that *tee* relates to a T-shirt or even solely to the letter *T*. The latter may indicate that it's a variation of an older phrase *to a tittle*, which means "down to a very small part of something."

Chapter 11

HORSE RACING

"We're a dark horse—a dark beheaded horse."

—*Game of Thrones* cocreator David Benioff
during the 2011 Emmys race

Calling someone an *also-ran* sure is dismissive. The ego-diminishing phrase leaves you feeling like an afterthought in whatever enterprise didn't go right. Even the phrase's beginnings have a throwaway feel. The after-the-fact vibe was very much a part of the phrase's introduction to print. In the 1830s, British newspaper summaries of horse races trumpeted the top three finishers. Then, below all the positive press, was simply, "The following also ran" trailed by a list of the losers.

The term became so well known that before the end of the nineteenth century people were using it to describe humans who didn't perform at or near the top of a competition. If all this negativity is getting you down, here's one small bit of solace: for a slightly less pessimistic reference to an unsuccessful matter, you can always go with another colorful horse-racing saying for a disappointing result, *finishing out of the money*. Like *also-ran*, it represents missing out on finishing first (win), second (place), or third (show). Then again, maybe that's not much better.

BY A NOSE

America's unique emphasis on the equine proboscis (translation: the horse's schnoz) at the track led to the handy phrase *by a nose* to describe a tight result in all sorts of ventures.

The British used *the nose* to describe a tight finish in the eighteenth century. In a 1789 match race between the Earl of Derby's horse C.C. and the Duke of Grafton's Freebooter, the event was dubbed in a newspaper report as "a prodigiously fine race; the horses buckled all the way—and Freebooter won by about *half a nose*."

But it took the U.S. horse-racing community to elevate *the nose* to a term of art in racing. By the late nineteenth century, the body part was a formal designation for a type of victory. You could win by a head or a neck, or, for the tightest outcomes, by a nose. (Instead of relying on the snout, the British have historically opted for the term *short-head* for the razor-thin difference at the finish line.)

So how close is a nose-length victory? The answer is unknown, as no specific measurement is given to a by-a-nose win. As for those wondering about the frequency of such a dramatic finish, consider this: in the first 140 years of the Kentucky Derby, only nine horses won by a nose. In contrast, twenty-three champions have triumphed by a dominating four lengths or more.

Figuratively, the expression is far more common and can be found in print by the start of the 1900s.

CAUGHT FLAT-FOOTED

Obvious question: Horses have hooves, not feet, so how did this sport spawn such an expression? While instinctually this phrase feels like a boxing term, it apparently surfaced during the reign of the British monarch Queen Anne (1702–1714), according to language expert Robert Hendrickson. At the time, *flat-footed* was already being used to describe an equine condition wherein horses or other animals lacked the normal inner hollow area in their hooves, Hendrickson says. From there it became colloquial for horses that appeared to be almost standing in place at the start of a race (all hooves on the ground) rather than with hooves a-flying.

If Hendrickson is right, Americans weren't as quick to accept the phrase. The expression didn't show up in U.S. newspapers until the beginning of the twentieth century, and by then it was used in both a baseball setting and at the horse races.

A 1907 syndicated column written by the star pitcher Addie Joss talked about a fielder failing to cover a base because he was "caught flat-footed on the play." A year later, a *Washington Post* story applied the phrase to a horse's slow start. Whichever was first in American papers, baseball writers seemed to use it as often as horse-racing journalists. The expression's more natural affinity to humans—a species with actual feet—also led to its application in foot races and boxing before its metaphorical application for being unprepared or surprised came about.

Unexpected phrase from horse racing: Dead ringer

Used today to describe a person who's the spitting image of another, a *dead ringer* was firmly part of horse-racing parlance near the end of the nineteenth century.

At first blush, the expression makes some vague sense. *Dead* is still used as slang for being precisely spot-on (think *dead center* or *dead heat*). *Ringer* also remains common code for a substitute of greater quality (as in "Sweet—our rec basketball team just picked up a ringer with NBA experience"). Put them together and you can sort of see a phrase combining "exact" and "replacement" developing.

But how did *ringer* get its meaning? A popular thought is that the word descended from an old saying, *to ring the changes*, which was used to describe when a seller secretly provided an inferior product instead of the expected goods.

DARK HORSE

The term *dark horse* has nothing to do with the color of a steed's coat. In actuality, most horse-racing gamblers probably care little whether a horse they back is brown, black, or white. What matters most both now and when this phrase developed in the 1800s was an animal's lineage. It's the quest for that knowledge that gave us this expression.

This rings true (apologies) when you understand how it was used in its track context. In short, horses known as *dead ringers* were put in races by gamblers looking to cheat the system. The scam involved replacing a good-running horse with a nag lookalike just before post time. Those involved would then get good odds on another horse, knowing the supposed strong runner was anything but that.

Still, mysteries remain. It's unclear how our doppelganger use of *dead ringer* dropped the unscrupulous connotation from the races. And, as far as a *ringer* (of the nondead variety) goes, we don't know how the term developed into one in which the replacement was an improvement. Finally, did the phrase truly start in horse racing? Newspapers were talking about human look-alikes being dead ringers around the same time the expression was first being applied to horses.

Beginning in 1605, stud books were created to keep track of every bred horse's family tree. The reason: Genes are considered a highly important indicator of a horse's success. (Geek note: This is where the term *stud* comes from to describe a particularly adept, strong, or good-looking guy.) Despite this commitment to record keeping, there were instances when horses entered a contest with no identifiable backstory. For these history-less competitors, the term *dark horse* was created (as in the animal's record was dark and, therefore, unknown).

Many sources credit the novelist and future British Prime Minister Benjamin Disraeli with coining the expression. He did include it in his 1831 novel *The Young Duke*, but by then the phrase had existed for at least a decade. According to an 1822 report on the well-known Doncaster St. Leger horse races, it was "a fortunate event for betting men. What is termed an *outside* or a dark horse always tells well for the heavy betters."

In our time, *dark horse* is commonly used by pundits and journalists to portray a political longshot, who may actually be a viable candidate. James K. Polk, winner of the 1844 U.S. presidential election despite being a relative unknown, is often labeled the first dark horse candidate for that top job. By the late 1840s, the English were using the phrase figuratively as in this 1847 issue of London's *Express*: "Lord Elgin still rides a dark horse— to use a sporting phrase. . . . He keeps his own counsel, takes no one into his confidence, imparts his views to no one."

FIRST OUT OF THE GATE

"Break cleanly." That's what most jockeys are thinking when they're loaded into the starting gate before a horse race. The rider may not be sure he'll win, but if he can navigate clear of the narrow stall expertly, it'll give him a chance at glory. With that in mind, you can be sure that the first out of the gate in any given competition is breathing a heavy sigh of relief.

As a colloquial term for being number one to action, *first out of the gate* is relatively new, dating to the 1960s. Starting gates didn't become common in horse racing until a few decades into the twentieth century. Sure, people dabbled—in 45 BCE the Romans started chariot races at the Circus Maximus from *carceres* (translation: "prison stalls"), where the horses would be simultaneously freed at race time. In modern times, an Australian inventor fashioned his own version of gated stalls in 1894.

But for most of horse racing's long stretch of history, colts and fillies would typically start in one of two manners. Either they'd work their way to a spot on the starting line and wait for a simple rope or other barrier to drop or they'd just line up with no obstacle whatsoever and take off at the wave of a handkerchief.

The evenhanded mechanized stalls should have lured horse racing's sovereigns to this form of start from its inception. But there was hesitation, as some owners feared their horses would struggle in these confined areas. It was a fair concern. Enough mounts were squirrely in the gates that the label *post rogues* developed quickly for these animals.

Some even continued to fight for the old-fashioned "walk-up" race after gates became the norm. When the people's horse Seabiscuit took on Triple Crown winner War Admiral in their epic 1938 one-on-one affair, War Admiral's handlers insisted they start without gates. In a reminder that getting out first (even without a gate) doesn't always determine the result, the horses broke pretty evenly, but Seabiscuit ultimately won by four lengths.

Horse-betting language

Wagering on the horses is as old as Western civilization. Even Homer wrote in *The Illiad* about how the Greek hero Ajax and the Cretan leader Idomeneus ventured a side bet on the outcome of a chariot race (one of the objects being wagered: a cauldron).

In truth, while horse racing has long been known as the sport of kings, a better title might be "the pastime for gambling aristocracy." Beginning in the early seventeenth century, nearly every organized British race had some lord, earl, or monarch placing bets on his favorite mount. These horse contests were often one-on-one match races between two steeds, and bigwigs like Lord Buckingham, Lord Salisbury, and Lord Pembroke were all early players, staking cash on horses in the 1620s and 1630s.

But with the rise of formalized gambling, bookmakers' lingo had a particular impact on the English language. According to Roger Longrigg's *The History of Horse Racing*, laying various odds for success on every horse in a race— and giving everyday people the opportunity to get involved—emerged around 1804.

At its most basic, this gambling explosion led to the idea of *a run for your money*. Used today to mean "making a legitimate challenge," it originally described wagering on a certain horse. Per London's *Morning Post* in 1839: "Several individuals . . . had backed the horse, and . . . decided to have a run for their money." (By the 1850s, it took on the added meaning of getting good value for your investment at the track.)

The more exacting math of varying odds spawned a number of expressions as well. An obvious one was *odds-on favorite*, which showed up in print in England by the 1870s (an 1877 issue of London's *Daily News* talked about a horse named Adieu being the "odds-on favourite" for a steeplechase meet).

In the United States, strategies for getting the most out of your betting options could have filled an idiomatic artesian well. *Playing the field*, which would eventually be used for dabbling with a broad range of dating possibilities, was shorthand in the 1880s for laying money down on every horse but the favorite. *Across the board*, which is used today as an expression for being wide-reaching, was originally used in the first decade of the twentieth century for putting down equal money on a horse to come in first, second, or third (commonly known as win, place, or show). At the end of the nineteenth century, that magical top-three result already had its own expression—being *in the money*. Later, it became a way to trumpet a financial windfall to the world at large. Of course, correctly picking all three top finishers also earned the *trifecta* moniker in the 1970s.

HANDS DOWN

The job of a jockey is a tough one. You're jostling with opponents while trying to control a speed-hungry animal galloping at a breakneck pace. To do this, two of your biggest tools are the reins and the whip, and to be at the ready in case he needs either one, a rider must have his hands up. (In particular, the hand must go high before using the whip to encourage a horse to giddyup.) But on those magic occasions when a horse has broken free from the pack and is cruising to victory, a jockey can lighten up on these items and, literally, put his hands down.

In an 1852 issue of the newspaper *Bell's Life in London and Sporting Chronicle*, a writer explained the importance of hand location in this context: "The Cup on the second day gave us a . . . race between the winning Storyteller and Kate," the report started. "The latter might have done better had the [jockey] been permitted to allow the mare to go in front with his hands down instead of pulling and hauling the animal as he did, by which much ground was lost."

With the phrase commonly in London papers in the middle of the 1800s (the cosmopolitan set loved their horse-racing coverage), it had little trouble earning a place as a wider expression for ease or minimal effort required. The *British Almanac* employed it that way in 1866: "It is a contest between Red-tape and the House of Commons, in which Red-tape will win, hands down."

HAVE A HORSE IN THE RACE

So that you're ready with a cheeky response next time somebody asks whether you have *a horse in the race*, let's talk about the literal costs for such a commitment. If you're mostly interested in just throwing some unknown mount into a local competition, you can pick up a horse for as little as $4,000. But if you're eyeing the big time and want a steed that could be a strong contender for a crown jewel event like the Kentucky Derby, the price tag typically balloons to between $200,000 and $2 million. As for upkeep, the outlay for maintaining a thoroughbred is around $35,000 annually.

Of course, when most people ask if you have a horse in the race nowadays, they're probably not thinking about equestrian competitions. They want to know who you're supporting in any sort of competitive undertaking—be it sports or otherwise. (Still, at least you're equipped now with the nuts-and-bolts meaning of the real thing.)

The phrase was used in the nineteenth century but appears to have gotten its metaphorical meaning mid-twentieth century in the political realm. In 1950, *The Cedar Rapids Gazette* in Iowa slipped it in while discussing state politics and Lieutenant Governor Kenneth A. Evans. The paper wrote: "If Evans gets the encouragement he feels he needs to run, each faction of the party will have a horse in the race."

Having a horse in the race does come from a long line of political idioms taken from the track. This section is full of them (for example, check out "Running mate" on page 156). Others include seeing the *horse race* as a parallel for an election fight; *backing the wrong horse* for choosing a losing candidate; *in the running* for a politician with a shot (or *out of the running* for a failed attempt); and *too close to call* for an unknown political outcome. (Geek note: *Backing a horse*—wrong or right—is among the oldest of these phrases, with many crediting William Shakespeare for its creation.)

Track or racecourse?

In the nineteenth century, Americans were widely known for plain-talking compared to their cousins on the other side of the Atlantic. The term for horse-racing venues is an example. In Britain, they were known as smooth-sounding *racecourses*, but, for the most part, in the United States, folks simply called them *tracks* (some snooty American locales were dubbed racecourses—like the one in Saratoga—but the more popular word was *track*).

Like the ultra-pithy name itself, the American horse-racing track was typically straightforward: oval shaped, with a dirt surface, and run counterclockwise. In contrast, British racecourses were a mixed bag of terrains (flat or rolling), shapes (ovals, straights, switchbacks, triangles), directions (right or left bends), styles (steeplechase or straight-up running courses), and lengths.

But when it comes to language, it's the United States' uniform track that has the richest contribution. British racecourses can claim the modestly used idiom *horses for courses* (meaning certain people are best suited for certain activities), but the American track trumps that with such powerhouse phrases as *inside track, track record,* and *fast track*.

While we can't be positive horse-racing tracks sprung all these metaphors—after all, sprinting and distance running sites were also known as tracks in the 1800s—there is some good support for the equine influence.

There's persuasive horse-racing provenance indicating that having an inside track (as in holding an edge) was from the horse world. An 1852 dispatch in the *Indiana State Sentinel* about Democratic Party leadership politics in Washington explained, "We must trot out our best horse to win the race. . . . Gen[eral Lewis] Cass is now full three lengths ahead and he has the inside track as against [James] Buchanan." This early idiomatic example clearly gives the saying to the horses.

Track record's starting point is less certain. During the nineteenth century, horse-racing journalists would praise horses who set track records (as in course-specific time standards), but achievers in track and field received the same kudos. Nonetheless, the expression's modern figurative definition—a history of performance, which can run the spectrum from perfect to poor—points to the horses. Good or bad track records are used by gamblers to decide when to lay bets, but we don't say runners establish terrible track records if they set disappointing new times at venues.

As for *fast track*, the *Oxford English Dictionary* credits firm and speedy horse-track conditions for its ultimate use when describing a person skyrocketing to success. Although, it's possible the term actually comes from railroads, where the expressions being *on track* or on the *right* or *wrong track* likely got their starts.

There's little doubt that horse racing gave the phrase *home stretch* (also known as the *final stretch*) its mass appeal. For most sports fans of a certain age, when the expression is mentioned in the context of horse racing, you can almost hear a nasally voice shouting, "And coming into the home stretch, it's Shammy Davis and Pants on Fire going neck and neck."* (Or, if you're a follower of the great announcer Dave Johnson, he tweaked the phrase slightly with his signature line, "And down the stretch they come!")

And, yet, whoever invented it for the final leg of a race was on to more than just the horses, because it didn't take long for the phrase to spread throughout sports and the world at large. (Interestingly, the British version of this American term, *home straight*, has never enjoyed the same appeal.)

Home stretch can be found in horse-racing reports by 1841, but within a little more than a decade, it was showing up in stories about foot races. Yachting and rowing followed, and baseball also took it before the end of the 1800s to mark the final push of games in a season.

As for nonsports territories, *home stretch* was in play in the 1860s for a broad variety of purposes, from the moments leading up to a legislative vote to the waning days of the corn-growing season.

---

*These are both real horses that competed in the Kentucky Derby; Shammy Davis came in twelfth (out of thirteen) in 1990, and Pants on Fire placed ninth (out of nineteen) in 2011. If you are reading this, you'll also be happy to know that Read the Footnotes came in seventh (out of eighteen) at the 2004 event.

NECK AND NECK

Watching two horses straining stride-for-stride in a race is exhilarating. And if you want to best capture the beauty of that moment, you should hone in on the horses' necks as they labor in unison down the track. It's a compelling sight and, understandably, gave rise to the expression *neck and neck*.

The phrase first showed up at races in 1672, according to the *Oxford English Dictionary*. The *neck* has long been in the track vernacular, not only as a body part, but also as a descriptor for the third-shortest distance that a thoroughbred can win by—after a nose (see "By a nose" on page 138) and a head. Idiomatically, *neck and neck* was being used in England by the opening of the 1800s to explain a close comparison or competition.

Here's a little trivia for your next day at the races: if you do focus on the horses' necks in a tight duel, you'll see more of the jockey than onlookers from a bygone era did. In the late nineteenth century, jockeys shortened their stirrups and began crouching over the necks of their horses. While it may distract from the drama of a pulsing neck-and-neck race, the repositioning did help revolutionize the sport, taking some of the rider's weight off their mounts. This improved race times by 5 to 7 percent.

OFF TO THE RACES

Long before there were courtside seats for Los Angeles Lakers games or the royal box at Wimbledon, if you wanted to see and be seen at a sporting event you simply had to go *off to the races*.

Back in the early and mid-1800s, there were no year-round tracks and competitions were primarily organized for the upper crust. Horse racing occurred at "meetings," which were like modern-day conventions taking place at specified times with lots of hoopla. These were such fancy affairs (sorry, no T-shirts or flip-flops) that late-nineteenth-century attire at the Royal Ascot horse race in England inspired the name for those fancy neckerchiefs known as ascots.

To be *off to the races* meant you were part of the elite, and the saying—and practice—weren't just about being British. In 1869, the *Melbourne Argus* wrote about how members of society in that Australian city went "off to the races." Upon their return,

Unexpected phrase from horse racing: Free-for-all

In modern speech, a *free-for-all* suggests chaos, but that wasn't the intention when horse-racing folks coined the term in the mid-1700s. Instead, free-for-alls were events that provided exactly what they claimed—a contest that was free for all who wanted to enter. Well, in truth, many of these races had restrictions, so they'd often be free for all *except* for those who hadn't paid a subscription to the track or *except* for a horse who'd won a large purse recently. Sometimes, it was free for all mounts of a certain age.

While the expression came from England, Americans welcomed it. It became common in the nineteenth century the writer wondered whether a load of "boisterous . . . mirth" was "solely attributable to the effects of horse-racing."

In 1865, a *Boston Post* dispatch about Paris's Longchamps Racecourse gave more insight into preparation for the races. "The day is wearing on—the afternoon is advancing, quick, quick—the new bonnet with the steel tassels—the parasol with the steel spangles—off to the races at Longchamps—not a minute must be lost!" The takeaway: You better look good and avoid being late for these shindigs. You could also expect to eat well. One 1840 British poem talked about going off to

when tracks often offered some free-for-all races. Other types of meets—like foot races—were also dubbed *free-for-all*.

It's from these U.S. roots that the phrase started to get its gritty meaning in the second half of the 1800s. Specifically, some early references used it to describe a raucous brawl. For example, in 1881, street melees from Las Mila, New Mexico, to Waldron, Indiana, were being tagged in newspapers as a "free-for-all fight."

How the benign notion of "no entry fee" morphed into "crazy fights" can't be explained here other than to note that they both have an uncontrolled nature to them. Over time, free-for-alls have maintained that unrestrained quality when applied to all sorts of other activities. Just ask a manager at a big box electronics store on Black Friday.

the races to eat lobster salad and prime Newcastle salmon and drink Champagne.

Before the end of the nineteenth century, the phrase's straightforward meaning was picked up for embarking on all sorts of goings-on. (Side note: If you want a similar racing expression with a little more oomph there's *off and running* or *off to a flying start*). Sadly, *off to the races* did lose its posh feel when others took it for more banal purposes. Proof positive: A figurative reference in an 1894 article from the *Boston Sunday Globe* came in a story about a tugboat. I doubt they had any Champagne onboard.

PEE LIKE A RACEHORSE

This idiom begs the question: is there something actually unique about a racehorse's urinary habits? The short answer is, in many cases, yes.

But before we get to that explanation, let's rewind to where this metaphor got its start. This all likely began with the statement *piss like a horse,* which can be found in writing by 1969. This allusion to a desire—or ability—to relieve oneself in epic proportions makes a lot of sense. A horse urinates between 1.5 and 2 gallons a day. In comparison, depending on one's liquid intake, a human produces about 1.5 quarts a day.

The substitution of a racehorse for your everyday equine in the phrase appears to have taken hold sometime in the 1980s and was popular enough in the following decade for esteemed authors like Stephen King (in *The Green Mile*) and David Foster Wallace (in *Infinite Jest*) to use it. (For those wondering, the more genteel *pee like a racehorse* also popped up in the 1990s.)

Because early references to this phrase don't suggest a knowledge of the inner workings of the horse-racing industry, it's possible the upgrade to racehorses was simply a literary flourish. Nevertheless, it's worth noting that in the 1970s, many trainers began giving racehorses a drug called Lasix (furosemide). Ostensibly, it's supposed to serve as anti-bleeding medication, but it also works as a diuretic, leading the animals to pee even more than your average horse. We can't be certain, but perhaps an observant fan of the races elevated this idiom.

PHOTO FINISH

If you don't believe language makes a difference in perception, contemplate the *photo finish*. When devices aimed at accurately identifying horse-racing winners began being installed at racetracks in the mid-1930s, they were often labeled as either the *electric eye* or the *camera eye* (cue Big Brother).

Mercifully, a marketing department (or maybe it was somebody in sales) figured out the less invasive and more exciting term *photo finish*. It didn't take long before it became the prime choice when referring to these contraptions.

Southern California's Santa Anita Park, which opened in December 1934, was the first high-profile racetrack to regularly utilize the photo finish. Within two years, it had spread to racing hotbeds in New York, Illinois, Maryland, and elsewhere. And why wouldn't they? Dishonesty is a problem horse racing has always battled (see "Shoo-in" on page 157 and "Dead ringer" on page 140). Photographic evidence of race results wouldn't wholly solve that issue, but it couldn't hurt.

The smart person who coined *photo finish* should have gotten a commission because the term almost instantaneously found a home in other sports. While horse-racing stories of photo finishes dominated newspaper sports pages, rowing and road racing also used the process to identify victors. Luckily, these other sports were smart enough not to call it an "electric-eye result." The more figurative use of the expression (to indicate a very close call) was in use by the 1940s.

RUNNING MATE

Many politicians are ambivalent about a *running mate,* thinking of that person as something like an extra arm. Sure, conceptually, the add-on could be helpful, but under most circumstances the addition is an awkward and completely useless part.

Back in 1730, Scottish poet James Thomson was far less uncertain about a running mate's value. He employed the expression as part of his epic poem *The Seasons.* Talking about the sounds of summer, he mused, "Sweeping with shadowy gust the fields of corn; while the quail clamors for his running mate."

Although Thomson was a pretty well-known poet in his day (the man did write the lyrics for *Rule, Britannia*), *running mate* didn't gain a toehold in the vernacular. Instead, we got the expression from the horse-racing community, which appears to have independently developed it more than one hundred years later.

In the 1850s, trotting matches were a popular style of harness racing that required an extra horse. Basically, the additional animal would be coupled to the competing horse and would set a speed the primary steed was required to follow. A horse named Ethan Allen was one of the great practitioners of this discipline, and his performance at a Long Island competition in 1859 was so newsworthy that it reached papers from Burlington, Iowa, to London, England.

These dispatches discussed how Ethan Allen and his opponent Lantern were each harnessed to a *running mate.*

As is the case in some presidential elections, Lantern failed in a heat because he "suffered under the disadvantage of having his running mate give up," according to a London paper. Racing wags liked the term, and it would subsequently be applied to training horses brought in to help thoroughbreds improve their performances.

Unlike Thomson's effort, this usage was so inviting that by the late 1860s it was widely used to depict an associate with a certain role (primarily in politics) or even a concept that went hand-in-hand with something, as in this example from an 1872 Louisiana education report, "Progress is the running mate to Time."

SHOO-IN

We shoo flies away and shoo kids into bed, but in the late nineteenth century, a lot of money could illicitly change hands with a well-planned *shoo-in* at the racetrack.

Horse-racing's notion of a shoo-in was likely created by jockeys or gamblers who were friends with the riders. This is how it worked: the riders in a given race would conspire to allow a weaker mount (who was given long odds) an easy path to victory. Behind the scenes, they'd wager on the chosen horse and make big bucks.

These schemes were called *shoo-ins* because of the imagery of other horses and their riders shooing the anointed winner across the finish line first. (Geek note: The term *shoo* has been around in a slightly different spelling since the seventeenth century and means *to drive away*. For those wondering, if you write it *shoe-in*, you're just misspelling the phrase.)

The expression was common enough by the 1890s that the *Washington Post* talked about a failed effort of this type in its

December 20, 1896, edition as a "'shoo in' that didn't 'shoo'";
the next day the *Post* followed up with another article on the
topic. "It is my intention to prevent an attempt at a shoo-in,"
the track in question's proprietor Judge Carter Hall said. "If I
had overlooked that trickery . . . the track might have suffered
irreparable injury. The public that patronizes racing is getting
wiser every day, and you can't fool with it."

A brief game changer: Bullfighting and rodeo

For fiction writers, busting out a man-versus-animal scenario
is a great device for drama. And while there are tons of
dangerous options (hello, *Jaws*), very few beasts (if any)
have a more ritualized—and romanticized—history in human
combat than the bull. This is most notable in Spain, where
the sport of bullfighting has long been considered a trusty
analogy for life's trials.

From the bullring comes *the moment of truth* to indicate
a make-or-break instant, as well as *mano a mano* for a head-
to-head confrontation (even though it translates to "hand-to-
hand"). *The moment of truth* ("*el momento de la verdad*")
describes when the bullfighter is on the verge of killing the
bull, and *mano a mano* applies to a competition between two
bullfighters. For many English speakers, these phrases were
introduced by Ernest Hemingway who discussed both in
his writing.

Alas, despite the judge's efforts—and, no doubt, the work of others—these scams continued to be a regular part of mischief in the sport. In 1909, one of the pastime's most popular venues, Santa Anita Park in Arcadia, California, got press for foiling a planned shoo-in.

With major writers like Damon Runyon using the phrase in their writing, it was just a matter of time before it migrated

One bullfighting element that is often mistakenly assumed to be a metaphorical touchstone is the *muleta*, which is a red cape that matadors use with the bulls while the crowd yells *olé*. Ironically, the animals are color-blind, so it's the movement and not the color that gets them going. For this reason, it makes sense that the expression *seeing red* for being seriously angry appears to have different roots.

A little closer to home (for Americans), another bull-oriented experience, the rodeo, spawned the expression *this isn't my first rodeo*, which commonly reflects having know-how in an activity—a very necessary trait for those planning to ride a bull. Not from the rodeo is *taking the bull by the horns*. That term, which reflects tackling a tough situation head-on, is really much older. It dates to at least 1711, when *Gulliver's Travels* writer Jonathan Swift used it idiomatically in another volume of his writing.

elsewhere. Most notably, the term became a political staple by the 1930s. But surprisingly, considering the election game's own propensity for crooked dealings, the idiom only retained the sure winner meaning and not the criminal intent behind the result.

STRAIGHT FROM THE HORSE'S MOUTH

First, let's clear up any potential misconceptions. *Straight from the horse's mouth* doesn't involve the popular 1960s talking-horse comedy, *Mister Ed*. It also has nothing to do with the age-old maxim, *Don't look a gift horse in the mouth*. Instead, the origin of—or at least the inspiration for—this expression came from the type of wise guys you'd find in the musical *Guys and Dolls*. You know, the gents wearing sharp suits and speaking fast out of the side of their mouths.

The phrase can be found in print by the 1910s to describe a guy who has horse-gambling inside info that is the real deal. By the following decade it was a well-established phrase spouted not only by those of a seedier ilk but also by regular people. The figure of speech was pervasive enough that a 1920 newswire story from Berlin talked about how locals were "reading the dope straight from the horse's mouth, from the [latest horse-racing] tipping papers."

Not long after, the saying became common for having any sort of information on the utmost authority. In 1931, author Aldous Huxley famously nudged the expression's linguistic standing along when he included it multiple times in his classic dystopian novel *Brave New World*. "A troop of newly arrived students, very young, pink and callow, followed nervously, rather abjectly, at the Director's heels," he wrote. "Each of them carried a notebook, in which whenever the great man spoke, he desperately scribbled. Straight from the horse's mouth."

UNDER THE WIRE

Before cameras were stationed at the finish line (see "Photo finish" on page 154), the result of a race could be very hard to discern. When you have horses running in the vicinity of forty miles per hour, and it's a close contest, a race can be a blur of colors and body parts right to the very end.

Recognizing this difficulty, American track organizers in the nineteenth century needed a little something extra to clarify a winner. They came up with a wire that would hang over the finish line. While it wasn't as technologically useful as photography became in the future, it did offer some help. It also served as a font for catchphrases.

By the 1860s, *down to the wire* was common in newsprint to reflect a race that wasn't decided until the last possible gallop. Around the same time, *under the wire* signaled when a horse had won. An example: "Secretariat triumphed, crossing under the wire first." Not long after, commentators began gushing about a *wire-to-wire* victory when a horse led a race from start to finish (as the wire also represented the starting point back then).

While *wire-to-wire* retained that dominant meaning in figurative terms (winning wire-to-wire is a start-to-finish success anywhere), *down to the wire* and *under the wire* have changed slightly. Rather than focusing on winning or losing, the two expressions' off-the-track emphasis is on the time element. In other words, if you took an assignment down to the wire, you've left it to the last possible moment. If you've finished just under the wire, you've satisfied your commitment in the nick of time. There aren't necessarily winners or losers. Then again, even if the work isn't good, completing it may be victory enough.

In the days preceding pristine oval tracks, horse racing had some pretty wide-open styles of competing. None may have been more outlandish than the wild-goose chase.

Despite what it sounds like, I can assure you no geese were harmed in the enjoyment of this game. Here's how it worked: One rider would gallop out front, the other participants in hot pursuit. They'd take off in an open field and, after a set distance, the lead would look to shake the pack. To do so he could dart wildly in any direction he wanted. Not only was the group required to follow but they also needed to do so in a set formation and at a set distance (they supposedly looked like a flock of geese, hence the name). If a rider failed to meet his spatial obligations, a judge riding nearby would whip the transgressor.

This type of follow-the-leader racing was common enough in the seventeenth century that a 1621 play was called *The Wild Goose Chase*. But it existed before then because William Shakespeare figuratively tweaked the haphazard nature of the proceedings in *Romeo and Juliet*, which is thought to have been written in the 1590s. "Nay, if our wits run the wild-goose chase, I am done," Mercutio said to Romeo, "for thou hast more of the wild goose in one of thy wits than, I am sure, I have in my whole five."

As goes Shakespeare, so go other writers, and the colloquial use of the phrase showed up regularly to illustrate a quixotic task or path. Among those who wisely used it was the novelist Nathaniel Hawthorne, who wrote in 1851: "Happiness in this world, when it comes, comes incidentally. Make it the object of pursuit, and it leads us a wild-goose chase, and is never attained."

Chapter 12

TENNIS

"A shutdown of our government would be
wildly irresponsible. It would be an
unforced error that saps the momentum
we've worked so hard to build."

—President Barack Obama in September 2015

In a shocking example of linguistic delay, the classic expression *the ball is in your court* didn't emerge until the mid-twentieth century—even though the first tennis courts date back to medieval Europe. No doubt, the sport was a lot different back then. The original version was called "real tennis," and there were no racquets (it was a hand-smacking game). Still, people were creating courts, and, while the balls looked different than

A brief game changer: Badminton

Newsflash for parents: When encouraging your hardworking kiddos to *keep it up* in school or sports, please note you're basically giving them an old rallying cry for partying. In his 1788 reference guide *A Classical Dictionary of the Vulgar Tongue*, writer Francis Grose defined the idiomatic phrase as "To keep it up, to prolong a debauch. We kept it up finely last night. . . ."

As naughty as its idiomatic beginnings might be, the expression actually started very innocently with a proto-version of badminton called battledore and shuttlecock. This simple pastime was developed in the fourteenth century and grew into a pretty popular sport by the start of the seventeenth century. The game was basic—each player had a racquet (called a battledore) and volleyed a shuttlecock, our fuzzy-covered rubber versions, the orbs did fly back and forth from one side of the court to the other.

Putting the ball into an opponent's court was a prime philosophical tenet ingrained in early tennis. Some believe the very word *tennis* comes from the French *tenez*, which is said to mean "take this." There is a bit of disagreement over this fact (there's no contemporaneous proof to support the claim), but we are sure that some players in the 1500s would cry out

which was made of cork with a series of goose feathers sticking out of one end.

Unlike badminton, there was no net and the basic goal was principally to keep it (the shuttlecock) up (in the air). The ambience here might be very juvenile, but the game was played by all types. When interned in the Tower of London for his supposed involvement in the 1605 Gunpowder Plot, the Earl of Northumberland allegedly played it, among other games, to pass the time.

The phrase's metaphorical meaning broadened beyond debauched benders by the start of the 1800s, but the will to *keep it up*—in battledore and shuttlecock terms—continued throughout that century. In 1830, one family reportedly set a record for keeping it up, volleying an impressive 2,117 consecutive times.

accipe or *excipe* in Latin (translation: "accept" or "take") when serving.

Conceptually, the idiom existed elsewhere in sports. By the seventeenth century, the soccer phrase *the ball is at one's feet*, which essentially means the same thing, was being kicked around.

Considering all that background, the enigma is why it took until around 1950 for the saying to show up in print. If that piques your curiosity, may I politely put the ball in your court to figure it out.

UNFORCED ERROR

Is there a statistic in sports that can make you feel worse than being told you've committed an *unforced error*? I mean, even the construction of "committing" the act feels like you've perpetrated a crime. Implicit in the phrase is the sense that the miscue was done in a vacuum. None of the inherent stress of competing in a pressure-packed athletic situation seems to exist with the unforced error. You just blew it.

That sense of self-inflicted blundering has been catnip for the political pundit class since the beginning of the twenty-first century. Talking heads on all sides of the political spectrum wield the expression to mock the seemingly very avoidable mistakes performed by politicians with opposing views.

As for the masochistic athletes who opened the door to this phrase, point your racquet at tennis players. The professional tennis community embraced the term in the 1970s. Though she wasn't the first, tennis champion Billie Jean King notably mentioned it in a book she coauthored in 1978 called *Tennis Love: A Parents' Guide to the Sport*. "Ah yes, the unforced error," she wrote. "The scourge of every human being who has ever stepped onto a tennis court."

The term took on formal meaning in 1982 when a company called Information and Display Systems used it as part of their first system of computerized tennis stats. The company officially defined the flub as an error not occurring "under any physical pressure as a result of the placement, pace, power, or spin of their opponent's stroke."

Within a few years, other activities were using it to admonish poor moves. In 1988, for instance, a British chess magazine reported that some masters of the board were keeping track of unforced errors in matches. Three years later, the *Los Angeles Times* pointed out that broadcasters at the Masters were noting golfers making unforced errors.

Tennis may be able to take credit for this idiom's popularity, but that doesn't mean every member of the sport believes it's necessary. "The forced error, unforced error count is always extremely tricky," tennis great Roger Federer told the *New York Times* in 2013. "I know, and my coaches know, what happened during the match, so I don't necessarily need stats to point things out."

Chapter 13

TRACK AND FIELD (RUNNING)

**"Once in a rare while, somebody comes along
who doesn't just raise the bar, they create an
entirely new standard of measurement."**

—Twitter CEO Dick Costolo on the death
of Apple cofounder Steve Jobs

HIT THE WALL

The dreaded metaphorical wall comes in many forms. It can smack you deep into a marathon when all your muscles give out, or it can arise when you've completely run out of gas trying to pull an all-nighter at the office.

By most accounts, *hitting the wall* started in the running community in the mid-1970s. For any athlete who has experienced that physiological moment of complete glycogen depletion, going headlong into a load of stacked bricks seems like an apropos analogy. In marathon races, the wall usually occurs somewhere between miles eighteen and twenty. By the early 1980s, idiomatic walls of all sorts were being erected in print.

Even before this potent image, there were descriptive words for abject exhaustion in stamina-requisite sports. By the 1930s, the term *bonk* had entered English as a general expression for a hard object striking a solid surface. In the 1950s, it was co-opted by endurance athletes (particularly bicyclists) to communicate utter fatigue.

HOP, SKIP, AND JUMP

The *hop, skip, and jump* or *hop, step, and jump* is a truly old-school sporting event, but a longstanding question is whether the inventors of the ancient Olympics embraced it. Antiquity sports scholars have long debated whether this variant of the long jump, which we now call the *triple jump*, was an original Olympic event.

Distances attributed to some classical-period competitors seem to align with what would be expected from the discipline. But a healthy contingent of naysayers believe the jump measurements are inaccurate and that these leapers were doing a more standard straight-up run and jump (aka the long jump).

Whatever the case, the combo has been well known throughout much of civilization's history. English speakers have been invoking the descriptive expression since at least the eighteenth century (and probably earlier). With literary giants like Sir Walter Scott and Robert Burns using it metaphorically in their writings in the 1700s, it was clearly a respectable turn of phrase for the literati.

Nevertheless, these masters of the quill were faced with one question: What should the phrase's figurative definition be? Most writers in the late 1700s used it to describe the cursory character of something. For example, in 1783, when the poet John Wolcot mentioned "a hop, and step, and jump mode of indicting," he seemed to refer to a slapdash indictment. Others, though, used it to mean a point-by-point approach. In a 1797 issue of London's *Monthly Mirror*, a writer counseled that "never can art or science be taught by hop, step and jump; from letter to letter."

Its modern symbolic meaning is typically rolled out in conversation to signify a short distance (as in "Let's go to the corner store. It's just a hop, skip, and jump away"). Knowing that greats in this sport can jump impressively long distances—like sixty feet—perhaps we should consider going back to one of the older definitions.

JUMP THE GUN

In the late nineteenth century, *jumping the gun* was considered a sign of a good runner. The phrase appears to have come from a similar phrase, *beating the pistol*, and publications talked about that as a smart strategy.

"Very often when athletes know that an incompetent pistol firer has charge of them, no attempt is made to hold the mark and all their thought and energies are bent on beating the pistol," an 1891 article in *Outing* magazine explained. "Half a dozen years ago, beating the pistol was such a common occurrence that an athlete was considered very slow if he did not do it."

Regardless of their shortcomings, race starters—and their pistols—continued to be essential staff when the modern Olympics began in 1896 (for those wondering, blanks or caps were the ammunition of choice). Naturally, the urge to anticipate the starting shot didn't diminish. Recognizing that problem, the watchmaker Omega came up with equipment in 1948 that could electronically detect an early start. But even before that high technology, *jumping the gun* had already become a pejorative for being too eager.

In reality, you couldn't blame runners trying to beat the gun, especially if they weren't in the lane closest to the pistol. In 2008, Canadian researchers published a study in the *Medicine & Science in Sports & Exercise* journal that concluded that, although starter pistols were connected to speakers behind runners—the theory being that everyone would hear the shot at the same time—the athlete in lane one was consistently getting off faster. The difference was a handful of milliseconds, but in a sprint that could be the difference maker.

Nowadays, a purely electronic mechanism is used, giving competitors one less excuse for jumping the gun.

MARATHON

Ask a Hollywood producer for two good rules for moviemaking, and you'll probably be told to ratchet up the drama and cut down the running time. Any studio chief who surveyed how the story arc for the *marathon* developed would surely say, "Mission accomplished."

The original tale of the Greek hero Pheidippides came from the great historian Herodotus, who put quill to parchment about sixty years after the famous Battle of Marathon in 490 BCE. Herodotus's retelling fades in on the great city-state Athens, recognizing it must engage a much more heavily manned Persian army than expected in armed conflict on the plains of Marathon. Looking for backup, the generals called on a legendary runner named Pheidippides to sprint to Sparta to plead for help.

Pheidippides took off by foot and covered 140 miles (or more, depending on the source you believe), getting to Sparta in two days. The Spartans agreed to help, but were delayed for religious reasons (they couldn't travel during a full moon). When they eventually got to the battle site, they saw the Athenians had already bravely repelled the Persians, making Pheidippides's journey a bit anticlimactic.

Future writers gave the whole thing a reboot. Hundreds of years later, authors Lucian and Plutarch each wrote about the event, whipping the plot into a different shape. The new story had the runner (who in some retellings wasn't named Pheidippides) scampering a much shorter distance—from Marathon to Athens. His job was to report that the Athenian army had prevailed against the Persians. After reporting, "Rejoice, we have won," he dropped dead. Fade to black. Cue applause.

We rely on this latter rendition—and its approximate distance from Marathon to Athens—today because that account became popular in the nineteenth century. Poet Robert Browning deserves a lot of credit for this. Seventeen years before the first modern Olympiad in 1896, he wrote a piece called *Pheidippides*, using the updated tale as inspiration. Its plot stuck with the organizers of the games.

The 26.2-mile distance for the marathon wasn't set until 1908, and its use as an expression for any sort of long experience began taking shape by 1915—though it doesn't appear to have been in regular idiomatic use until the middle of the twentieth century.

PASS THE BATON

The baton had a long history before it entered the sports world. The Scottish brought the word into the English language from the French in the sixteenth century, and for hundreds of years, it reflected a sticklike weapon or a staff that denoted power or authority. It was also used to describe an orchestra conductor's wandlike stick.

When it came to rebranding it as the shorter, cylindrical pipe-type thing relay runners pass along, it took some time for track officials to get on board. The ancient Olympics didn't have team racing, so only solo runners took part in 1896 at the inaugural modern Olympiad. That changed at the 1908 Olympics. But in that competition, instead of handing off an object, the running exchange was done with a touch.

Still, the concept of an item handoff did exist. Firefighters in the United States passed a red pennant from one runner to the next in relay races in the early 1890s, according to the book *Sports: The Complete Visual Reference*.

The Olympics finally relented and added the baton (sorry, no red flags) to its relay races at the 1912 event. That said, organizers may have been right to be leery. At those games in Stockholm, officials disqualified a number of teams for improper handoffs, leading to a lot of grousing.

As for this usage of the word *baton* and the creation of the phrase *passing the baton*, they were more easily adopted. They showed up regularly in newspaper stories about track races across the United States just after the 1912 Olympics.

Using the expression figuratively to indicate a handing off of responsibility was in print by 1930. The early definitions of *baton*—especially when talking about a rod of power or even a conductor's instrument—could have also inspired the idiom, but the timing of its popularity gives the inspiration from the track a leg up, so to speak.

= QUICK (OR SLOW) OUT OF THE BLOCKS =

In the first half of the twentieth century, it didn't matter whether you were *quick* or *slow out of the blocks*. Either way, it was a big problem.

You see, getting into any kind of blocks at the starting line—rather than digging toeholds in the dirt—was deemed unnatural. As far as old-timers were concerned, runners who wanted to use blocks were effectively seeking an artificial performance enhancer. While it wasn't steroids, using blocks gave between a 2.7-inch and a 2-foot advantage over the traditional starting method according to a well-publicized 1933 study performed in Iowa City.

Even before the eggheads got involved, people were nitpicking. In 1910, a *Boston Post* columnist voiced local disapproval about New York track men wanting to use blocks for indoor meets. When the great sprinter Howard Drew bounded out of blocks at an indoor competition in 1916, there was more grumbling. In fact, blocks were banned for outdoor competitions by international track and field officials until 1937 and didn't make it to the Olympics until 1948.

Not everyone was so negative about these devices. To this day, Australians laud sprinter Charlie Booth for devising a form of starting block in 1929. The story goes he trained at a dog track and was getting grief for digging toeholds that would endanger

A brief game changer: Unsportsmanlike language

Not all supposedly sporty phrases are what they seem. For example, *all-star* started in showbiz and *blitz* and *rookie* come to us from the military. Here are four popular terms that didn't develop on our favorite playing fields.

Boxing Day: This holiday, which originated in England, occurs annually on the first weekday after Christmas. Historically, it was a time when the wealthy bestowed gifts on the less well-off. There are many theories about how the event got its name. The most popular is that presents are often known as Christmas boxes in Great Britain, and the title came from there.

Have a ball: The meaning here comes from fancy dances. This usage of the word *ball* dates back to at least the 1500s and is derived from the French, who had a similar word they used the canines. So he fashioned a no-holes-necessary starting apparatus out of a T-bar and two blocks of wood.

Despite the Aussie enthusiasm, the pushback on blocks probably delayed this expression's metaphorical development. It really didn't take on broader meaning outside sports until the 1980s. Considering the phrases' snail-paced linguistic development, it's fairly appropriate that *slow out of the blocks* seems to have caught on first.

for a social gathering. The idea of throwing one of these festive events gave rise to this encouragement to have a fun time.

Keep the ball rolling: This phrase was popularized during the 1840 U.S. presidential race between William Henry Harrison and Martin Van Buren. Harrison supporters pushed huge balls (ten to twelve feet in diameter) covered with slogans from village to village in support of their candidate. The phrase may have been used before then, but these efforts to keep the ball rolling not only helped Harrison win the election but also boosted the expression.

On the rebound: Bouncing off one relationship and into another was coined before basketball creator James Naismith was even born. To catch a person—or more specifically a heart—*on* (or *in*) *the rebound*, could be found in writing by the 1830s.

Incidentally, the similar *quick off the mark* went idiomatic by the 1930s. If track inspired the phrase, its swifter rise is apropos as, with no blocks to speak of, there would have been less negativity surrounding it.

RAISE (OR LOWER) THE BAR

Oh, how I wish the origin of *raising the bar* involved the legendary tale of some magnificent drinking establishment's creation. Instead, we must satisfy ourselves with feats of athleticism from the pole vault and the high jump.

While the first pole-vaulters actually propelled themselves horizontally through the air as far as they could (think of it as a pole-aided long jump), both sports were raising bars—or lowering them for those too challenged—by the middle of the 1800s. In fact, these disciplines' bar-shifting antics became so popular that when the very first Olympics occurred in 1896, both were on the program.

The *raise-the-bar* expression can be found in British newspapers in the 1860s. Along with its sports usage, it also had a legal meaning, reflecting the removal of a barrier. So to raise the bar in that courtroom context generally meant taking away a statutory impediment.

But using it to represent increasing or decreasing a level of expectation is a twentieth-century construct that almost certainly drew inspiration from the sporting world. *Setting the bar higher* (or *lower*) are variations that also smack of leaping over loftily placed hurdles.

For the literal-minded, how far you raise the bar in track and field varies depending on the governing body and the discipline. In the high jump, it's usually done in 2 to 5 cm increments. The pole vault's minimum upward movement tends to be 5 cm.

Chapter 14

WRESTLING

**"Comedy is a very rough beat.
It's no holds barred, as it should be."**

–Comedienne Joan Rivers

GO TO THE MAT

Wrestlers who would *go to the mat* in the first half of the twentieth century faced two adversaries—the opposing grappler and the mat itself. Original mats were unhealthy inventions of canvas with straw or horsehair crammed inside. They were often lumpy, too hard to cushion a big fall, and difficult to keep clean.

Mat burns were common, and with sweat- and blood-soaked mats, there was always the chance you'd catch an infection. High-end clubs, like the New York Athletic Club, would set up two mats and overlay a carpet on each. The carpet covering would be frequently changed, solving the hygiene issue but presumably not the burns. In the 1950s, foam-based alternatives were being installed in gyms across the United States, vastly improving a wrestler's safety (at least when it came to the mat).

Saying *go to the mat* to express a wrestler's plan to tussle appeared in newspapers by the late 1890s. (An early example: An article in an 1897 Indianapolis paper read, "Burns will go to the mat weighing 142 pounds and Hale 147.") With wrestling's popularity growing at the beginning of the twentieth century, the idea of *going to the mat* being a metaphorical willingness to battle hard was ingrained by the 1910s.

NO HOLDS BARRED

When the term *no holds barred* entered the wrestling lexicon in the 1890s, the expression must have been nerve-rattling. Beyond the "stranglehold" (see page 185), there were numerous other scary-sounding wrestling forms of attack—known as holds—allowed if there were no holds barred: the cross-buttock, the flying mare, a punishing double chancery hold, and the still-discussed full nelson.

And yet, it was the prospect of seeing these maneuvers that made *no holds barred* a major draw in wrestling's formative days in America. Much like early boxing, freestyle wrestling was a bellicose attraction. While the more classical Greco-Roman code required that all holds be above the waist, freestyle permitted latching on just about anywhere. Often in the context of a traveling show, wrestlers would take on locals and, as a marketing ploy, amp up the interest by emphasizing this aggressive approach. In many ways, these fights were a lot like today's mixed martial arts (sadly, there was no octagon at the time).

With few rules, this was dangerous stuff, and some promoters began hedging their promises for free-for-all melees. For example, a Chicago prizefight in 1898 was hailed as "no holds barred, except throttling."

Even though moderating regulations became commonplace in wrestling, the freewheeling nature of the phrase allowed for an easy shift into common speech. In the 1910s, it was used by other sports—like baseball—to indicate a team going all out to win. By the next decade, it was applied to no-restriction efforts in most everything else.

By the way, for those who might consider no holds barred barbaric, there was another idiom-inducing form of scrapping that was far worse: *rough and tumble*. This type of unsanctioned brawling was far more *Fight Club* than proper boxing or wrestling and was best known in the eighteenth and nineteenth centuries as a brand of score-settling combat that included eye gouging. In the early twentieth century, the phrase began to represent less dangerous behavior that thankfully (one hopes) didn't regularly lead to gouging.

Okay, you're never going to find a proper wrestling match where somebody asks for submission by *saying uncle*. But if you happen upon an unlicensed kids' scuffle, you're bound to find some poor pinned soul being forced to yell the famed magic words.

Isn't it strange that we have to call for a relative when opponents want us to concede defeat? In 1980, a journal called *American Speech* took a crack at explaining it, claiming that it probably came

Wrestling feints

If you're *pinning down* a friend on a time for drinks or watching the computer guy troubleshoot a problem on your computer *catch as catch can* (in other words, by whatever means available or possible), wrestling likely played a role in putting those expressions in your head. Still, neither phrase began with its use on the mat.

Historically, the idea of *pinning down* had numerous meanings before being formally introduced in wrestling. To *pin down*, meaning to hold somebody to a promise, was in play by 1710. By 1718, the phrase was also used to specifically identify or describe an act or a characteristic. To pin down by conceptually putting people in a position where they couldn't maneuver (example: "The cavalry was pinned down in the valley") was in print by 1795.

from an old Irish word *anacol*, which meant an "act of protecting; deliverance; mercy."

This explanation didn't sit well with some word experts, who believe the phrase is an American colloquialism. (Since when do kids use archaic Irish when wrestling?) Instead, etymology expert Michael Quinion offered a more plausible—though still surprising—explanation: *crying uncle* came from a joke.

While physically pinning a person down existed in 1738 (though not in a wrestling match per se), the idea of holding both shoulder blades on the ground to win a grappling contest did emerge in the late nineteenth century, according to the *Oxford English Dictionary*.

Catch as catch can was the name of a popular nineteenth-century form of wrestling developed in Lancashire, England. Americans adopted the phrase at the end of the 1800s as a name for freestyle wrestling. These applications surely strengthened the phrase's place in the language, but the term was already being used before grapplers seized it. Originally, the phrase was *catch that catch may*. It was in the language as early as the late 1300s and had a similar idiomatic definition to the one we use today.

In around 1891, a humor piece started circulating in London newspapers about a man who bought a parrot. This guy tried to teach the bird to call him uncle. He implored his parrot to "say uncle." But he was unsuccessful and grew so frustrated that he began wringing the animal's neck. (Some retellings of the story said he got the parrot from a niece, accounting for the uncle reference.)

After a while, the thoroughly aggravated fellow threw the bird into a coop with ten prized fowls. Following a moment of contemplation, the man feared his parrot would be killed, so he went to retrieve the bird. When he returned he saw nine dead fowls and the parrot squeezing the neck of the tenth while exclaiming, "Say uncle!"

The joke was the era's version of a Jimmy Fallon viral YouTube video. By 1892, it had crossed the Atlantic, and American papers, ranging from large ones like the *New York World* to small outlets such as the *Mountain Democrat* in Placerville, California, picked it up. The joke was remarkable for its longevity. Editors were still running variations more than a decade after it originally appeared (apparently news travels slowly to Farmington, New Mexico, where the local paper ran it in 1908).

Forget archaic Irish: The joke's combination of "say uncle" along with the physical beat-down given by the parrot offers a more plausible gateway to the phrase being a mainstay in backyard wrestling matches, and beyond, for any act of capitulation.

STRANGLEHOLD

Before Hulk Hogan and Rowdy Roddy Piper, there was the wrestler Evan Lewis. Like Hulk and Rowdy—and the Iron Sheik, Macho Man Randy Savage, Andre the Giant, The Ultimate Warrior, and so many others in this line of work—Lewis sported a nickname: the Strangler.

The big difference between the Strangler and those other wrestlers mentioned is there was no stagecraft in what Lewis did. When he became America's first heavyweight wrestling champion in 1887, he earned his handle in a fair fight. And, he got it thanks to his signature move, the *stranglehold*.

In these early days of anything-goes wrestling (see "No holds barred" on page 180), very little was more vicious than the stranglehold. Case in point: At an 1892 fight in Bradford, Pennsylvania, a guy named W. E. Gibbs (aka the "Kansas demon") put his opponent Dennis Gallagher in a stranglehold so brutal that the crowd started yelling, "'Don't murder him!' 'Foul!' 'Let go of him!' and other exclamations [that] came from the horrified spectators." Gibbs was rendered unconscious by the maneuver, but was eventually revived.

Well, our friend the Strangler was the master of the move, which was also descriptively known as the *neck yoke*. Loved or hated but never ignored for his harsh tactics, Lewis was the talk of wrestling before the turn of the century and, as a result, the stranglehold's fame (or infamy, depending on whom you talked to) reached its zenith. But as Lewis faded at the end of the 1800s, so did his stranglehold. By the close of the next century's first decade, people found it too violent to stomach. According to a 1909 book called *The Complete Science of Wrestling*, the hold had been "very properly barred under almost every wrestling code."

Nevertheless, there was a legacy for Lewis's air-sucking headlock. Thanks in large part to the Strangler's exploits, the term's use as a catchall for complete control of a situation took hold at the beginning of the 1900s.

WRESTLING

The notion of *wrestling* (or in verb form, *to wrestle*) is probably as ancient as *Homo sapiens*. The physical activity was common enough in 3000 BCE that both Babylonian and Egyptian art depict it. The Greeks were fanatics, turning the activity into a centerpiece sport. At one point, their ancient Olympic version of the pentathlon included wrestling as a key event.

Not surprisingly, even before we had the English language as we know it, wrestling occurred on the British Isle. Seeing a need, wordsmiths developed a term for the act early on. Their linguistic seed was likely *wrest*, which was in the language by the year 1000 and meant "to twist or turn." To wrestle—as in to grapple on the ground—was being used by 1100. It must have sounded just right for the action because cognates existed in a host of archaic languages, including Old English (*wrǽstlian*), North Frisian (*wrassele*), Low German (*wrösseln*), and Middle Dutch (*worstelen*).

With sports metaphors being such a popular tool in language (heck, you're near the end of a whole book on them right now!), early English writers grabbed *wrestle* by the thirteenth century as a way to express striving "with or against difficulties, circumstances, forces, [or] personal feelings," according to the *Oxford English Dictionary*.

A brief game changer: Gymnastics

Language from gymnastics generally falls into a gray area. While we think of many of the sport's maneuvers when we use an idiomatic phrase, it's likely that they started in the entertainment world of acrobats. So if you show great effort by *bending over backward* to help another, or you're so thoroughly in love that you're *head over heels*, or you're so thrilled that you're *doing somersaults*, the phrases all appear to have come from traveling acrobatic exhibitions before reaching the sport of gymnastics. The same goes for the *springboard*, meaning "increasing a chance of success." (A side note: The springboard did originally start on dry land. It was used for vaulting before the end of the 1700s but didn't show up in print in conjunction with swimming until the mid-1800s.)

FREE AGENTS:
Unattached Sports Idioms and Words

Sports are about definitive outcomes. With some exceptions (soccer and ice hockey, please stand up), you'll have winners and losers at the end of an athletic contest.

Unfortunately, in the murky world of etymology, assigning victory isn't as easy. Some phrases and words are so generalized that they could apply to just about any game—I ask: What sport doesn't want *fair play*? Elsewhere, there are instances when multiple sports started using a given expression at around the same time, making it nearly impossible to award credit where credit is due.

This section picks up the slack. The following are idiomatic expressions and terms that don't have conclusive homes. Included are their figurative meanings and some insight into their often ambiguous origins.

All bets are off: All agreements or plans are void, creating uncertainty. This expression was used in relation to sports gambling in the early 1800s. You can find boxing references in newspapers relating to a bout being canceled in 1817. But it was also applied early on in relation to a pigeon-shooting contest (of all things), and, most likely, horse racing. Whether it was taken from other forms of betting (like cards or dice) is not known, but I'd wager it's probable. By 1845, it was being used figuratively.

Bad call and good call: A poor decision or thought, and a well-conceived idea or judgment, respectively. The concept of a call—as in a ruling—on a field of play dates back to at least the 1870s, when it was used by referees in rugby. But its idiomatic transition happened in the United States by about 1970, according to the *Oxford English Dictionary*. In the hundred years between the sports and metaphorical references, practically every athletic pursuit could boast good and bad calls, meaning that sports, in general, deserve paternity.

Benched (and on the bench, to bench): Relegated to an inactive status. As is the case with *on the sidelines* (see page 195), wherever you have a standard-size team, there are folks who are going to be banished to nonplaying roles. All the major North American team sports—baseball, basketball, football, and ice hockey—feature benches for those not in the action. The phrase entered the lexicon of games by the 1910s, and as baseball and football were the most popular pastimes then, they're the probable origin. But given that it didn't go idiomatic until the mid-twentieth century, all the above pursuits (and others) could have contributed.

Bowled over: Overwhelmed by something. Though it seems self-evident that *bowled over* got its start in bowling (hello, the word *bowl* is contained in the expression), there is no airtight evidence that ties the sport to the phrase. If you picked up a newspaper in London during the 1830s or 1840s, you'd find a number of sports stories discussing how a losing horse in a race was bowled over. You could also read about how a bowler (which is cricket-speak for what baseball calls a *pitcher*) bowled over an opposing batter. (In other words, the hitter was retired.) But you'd be hard-pressed to find the phrase in a bowling reference. By at least the nineteenth century (though I'd expect it has a longer history), the phrase had developed into an idiom.

Clear a hurdle: Overcoming an obstacle. This likely started in horse racing, where the steeplechase discipline was popular in nineteenth-century Britain. But foot racers, who have been leaping over obstacles since ancient times, might challenge that.

Dropped the ball: A mistake or an error. There are so many potential candidates for the starring ball in this phrase: rugby ball, baseball, football, you name it. There are even some options without a tie to sports, like balls that once served as gun ammunition or a large ball that was used to tell time at the Royal Observatory in Greenwich near London (although nearly all experts rule out the last one).

Fair play: Acting with respect and equity toward all involved. It's really hard to say whether sports inspired this phrase. Examples exist from the 1500s, and, most notably, William Shakespeare, who wrote at the end of that century and the start of the next, used *fair play* in a number of his plays. Now Shakespeare sure loved a good sport analogy. Just flip briefly through this book to find many instances, from "Bandy" (see page 74) to "There's the rub" (see page 106). Could *fair play* have been another example of him mining his sporting sense? It's possible.

Finish line and starting line: The location, point in time, or activity that marks completion or the beginning, respectively. A good guess suggests these phrases came from running races. But newspapers from the mid- to late 1800s, the period when the terms began to be used, included them in conjunction with not only tests of foot speed, but also yachting, rowing, and horse racing.

Front-runner: A leader or prime candidate. This phrase got its start in the United States, but who was the first to use *front-runn*er? The *Oxford English Dictionary*'s earliest citation is from 1914 and comes from auto racing. But a 1905 edition of the *Washington Post* applied the term to a horse named Nutcracker. Then there's foot racing, which would also be a natural birthplace for this expression.

Game changer and game changing: A situation-shifting person, act, or idea. These phrases appeared in U.S. newspapers by the 1960s to describe pivotal moments as well as key players in multiple sports, including football and basketball. An unscientific perusal of old papers indicates that *game changing* was the more popular expression in the twentieth century, but that *game changer* has come on strong—particularly in politics—in the 2000s.

Game face: Looking or acting with intensity and focus (as in "get your game face on"). This term was in use by 1950. The first known *game face*, according to a columnist at the *Wisconsin State Journal*, appeared on University of Minnesota football coach Bernie Berman's visage in the days before a contest against the University of Iowa. While the gridiron may have spawned it, the generic nature of the term suggests it was a general sports phrase before becoming idiomatic.

Game over: A situation where success appears hopeless; the end of any sort of event. Baseball articles described the end of a contest as "the game is over" in the 1880s. From there it was likely shortened to *game over*. In cricket, an *over* is a technical term for a certain segment of a match (a series of six balls bowled from one side of a pitch before switching ends), so it's possible that that sport was the inspiration. The versatile nature of the phrase also leaves the door open for other sports origins.

Game-time decision: A choice made just before an event commences. Personnel options in sports can be difficult, but it wasn't until the 1940s that use of this phrase to describe a last-minute pronouncement on a lineup entered the vernacular. It looks like it was first used in football but was picked up in most team sports well before becoming a popular idiom in the twenty-first century. Hence, its metaphorical inspiration could be baseball, basketball, or its probable originator, football.

Go the distance: Persevering until the very end. This phrase most likely started in horse racing, where it can be found from at least the 1840s. Still, you can't count out boxing, which was known for its marathon bouts during the same century and could have applied this expression as well (see "Go a few rounds" on page 113).

Ground rules: The basic principles of behavior or an activity. In the 1830s, people wrote about the ground rules of arithmetic and the ground rules of science, but our modern usage likely comes from a different type of ground—a playing field. Baseball was using the expression by the 1870s and probably first popularized it in the United States. (Think of a *ground-rule double* as a modern artifact to this usage.) But the term *ground* has a British feel to it, suggesting the phrase may have come to the United States via cricket or early forms of soccer. Then again, baseball linguists may have been motivated by math and science.

Grudge match: A competition fueled by previous hostilities (though modern idiomatic usage usually focuses more on a rematch of some sort). This expression showed up in a 1903 issue of the *New York Times* in a story on, get this, a handball competition. Not long after, articles could be found heralding boxing and wrestling events as grudge matches. Taking into account the aggressive nature of the expression, one would think it originally came from one of those contact sports.

Head fake: A maneuver done to deceive. Both football and basketball players were using this technique well before the twentieth-century's midpoint. Which athlete looked left and went right first, and from which sport, isn't exactly known, but football's longer history probably gives it the edge. Still, there's no surefire answer as to whether somebody on the gridiron had the wherewithal to name the move first.

Head in the game: Being focused and mentally present. This phrase was wielded idiomatically by the 1890s. (For instance, in August 1897, a small-town Iowa paper lauded a local businessman named J. S. "Jake" Bowder when he bartered for a drugstore: "Jake always keeps his head in the game and as usual made a very good thing on this trade.") As for its sports origin, both baseball and football references can be found in the same decade. The expression *old head in the game*, which described a veteran athlete, was also popular at the time and may have played a role in the development of the more recognizable usage.

Head start: To have an initial advantage. This expression was around in the nineteenth century. While we often connect it to running, horse racing is a more likely starting point, although hunting and boat racing also employed it before it entered everyday conversation in the latter part of the 1800s. If you think about it, some sort of equine action makes sense. After all, having a literal head start means something when the head is horizontal, as with horses; a head advantage would be vertical with humans.

Keeping score: Tabulating who is winning and losing in a figurative sense; also *knowing the score* for understanding where you stand in a situation. The word *score* has numerous meanings, and some might wonder whether these expressions actually relate to a musical piece. Indeed, a 1946 reference to *knowing the score* as being familiar with sheet music probably puts its origin outside the sports realm. But considering the winning and losing nature of keeping score—and the timing of its emergence (twentieth century)—the expression was likely instigated by action on a field or in a stadium.

Keeping your eye on the ball: Staying focused. This could have easily first been said by a coach to an athlete in cricket, golf, soccer, tennis, rugby, or baseball. That said, our earliest reference comes from an 1860 book called *Ernest Bracebridge or, Schoolboy Days*, which mentioned how a player "kept his eye on the ball, and hit it so fairly that he sent it flying away to a considerable distance" during a game of rounders (a British predecessor to baseball). In 1865, the *Brooklyn Eagle* ran a story about baseball that was syndicated to newspapers across the country. In it, the writer explained that to follow baseball, "all you have to do is to keep your eye on the ball." The first idiomatic instances appear to have come out of America. A June 25, 1917, ad in the *Washington Post* for a men's clothier laid out the analogy: "The man who looks at the price mark instead of the suit is like the ball or tennis player who lets his eye wander from the ball. Keep your eye on the ball—look at what you pay for."

Level playing field: A state of equality in a situation. While you can find municipalities in the early 1900s worried about erecting level playing fields for local kids, this metaphor didn't rise until the late 1970s, leaving it an open question whether any particular type of playing field was in the anonymous coiner's mind. Experts believe the idiom was created in the United States. If that's true, football or baseball (along with the aforementioned all-purpose kids' playgrounds) would be top possibilities for sources.

Make a play: To go after something (or someone) with the hopes of securing it. Early baseball lingo included the phrase *making a play* to portray a properly executed defensive maneuver. By 1905, *making a play* off the field was being used but with a different connotation. When someone said, "I'm making a play for that job," an air of uncertainty surrounded the result. That tweaked meaning leaves some doubt about whether baseball deserves the credit here.

Oddball: A strange, unconventional, or eccentric person. Like many ball idioms, provenance is generally elusive for *oddball*. This word entered the English lexicon in the mid-1940s. In 1945, one newspaper referred to Frankie Kovacs, a colorful tennis player, by the nickname "Oddball." Whether Kovacs was an early recipient of this emerging term or had some hand in its growth isn't clear. Either way, he was a good pick for the sobriquet as the man was quite unconventional. Stories say he once threw three balls in the air during a serve, hitting the middle one for an ace. He also sat down on the court mid-match at least once.

On the sideline(s): Being marginalized from or unable to take part in the action. The term *sideline* was first used in the language of British sports such as soccer, rugby, and tennis. But, for the most part, it was ultimately disregarded in soccer and rugby parlance in favor of the word *touchline*. As a result, the expression appears to have materialized in the United States at the dawn of the twentieth century. Credit for it should probably go to football writers, who often used the phrase early on. Still, tennis, where players talked about the operative sidelines first, is also a potential birthplace. It was used figuratively by the end of the first decade of the 1900s.

On your game: Executing at one's best. Billiards seems to have gotten this expression started in the 1840s. Writers on more than one occasion during that decade talked about being *on* or *off one's game* in the context of pool. Nevertheless, the generic nature of the phrase allowed reporters to pick it up as an expression for lauding athletes of nearly any discipline during the more than a century before it developed into a nonsports part of language in the 1960s.

Playing catch-up: Attempting to make up for lost time. At the start of the 1930s, variations of the phrase can be found—like a January 1930 football game report from a Decatur, Illinois, paper saying a team was "forced into hard play to catch up." Later in the decade, the phrase as we know it was in use in a *Wichita* (Texas) *Daily Times* report on an August 1935 softball tournament. Interestingly, that same Texas paper used the expression idiomatically in June 1940, describing how "the allies play catch-up so much of the time" during the early days of World War II.

Playing the angles: Maximizing one's position based on the possible scenarios in a situation; also *knowing all the angles* for being prepared for every eventuality. Both expressions come from the early twentieth century, with *knowing all the angles* being of a slightly older vintage. Billiards is the best candidate for popularizing these phrases in a sporting sense, but other games, including baseball and squash, were associated with them early on. Also, nonsports sources like architecture may have had a role in *knowing all the angle*'s conception.

Race against time: Working against a deadline; also, *race against the clock*, with similar meaning. The combo of *against* and *time* to reflect a type of racing has shown up in print since the mid-1700s. While horses most often competed under the clock, bicyclists, runners, and even ice skaters were participating in timed matches by the nineteenth century. In July 1809, the *Sporting Magazine* even reported on an "Ass race against Time." The wager was whether the donkey could go fourteen miles in less than two hours. The animal (with a jockey on board) did it with nearly twenty minutes to spare.

Run its course: To reach an end point or to complete development without outside meddling. The word *course* to describe a race venue can be found in print dating back to the 1300s, according to the *Oxford English Dictionary*. So when the *run its course* construction popped up in the 1400s, the combo was quite possibly athletically inspired. Nevertheless, it doesn't appear to be a sports term per se, as *run its course*—in writing at least—was purely an idiomatic expression from its beginning. If it was used in the sports world, it probably came from horse racing with the "its" representing a horse. (For those who think this phrase began in the medical field—as in a course of antibiotics— think again. That usage for *course* didn't emerge until the seventeenth century.)

Run out the clock: To stall or waste time in order to get a desired result. During the 1940s, commentators discussing America's two most popular time-sensitive team sports— football and basketball—started talking about *running out the clock*. One can only imagine that teams leading a game in either sport would have stalled in the waning moments of a contest well before the 1940s. But that was the decade the phrase took off, and based on the amount of early press, football coaches opted for this tactic more often than their hoops counterparts. Then again, maybe basketball chieftains were a bit better at hiding their use of the strategy.

Runoff: Political moments requiring additional electioneering to settle a race between top vote-getting candidates. *Runoff* was used by the mid-1800s when either foot or horse races required an additional contest to decide a winner following a dead heat. It entered politics in the United States by the beginning of the 1900s.

Run-up, the: The period of time leading up to an event. A bowler does a run-up in cricket, and a long jumper performs one before taking a big leap. Both of those disciplines used this phrase before it developed into a colloquial expression for the all-important prep phase before a big day. Still, if you're looking for the first sport to unveil the term, it's most likely greyhound racing. The *run-up* is jargon for the section that dogs run before the first turn in a race. It was in use by the 1830s. (Geek note: *Runner-up* also comes from dog racing.)

Score, to: To make a successful point in a discussion or debate, to obtain intimate relations with another, or to acquire something coveted (often used in relation to illicit activity). *Scoring* is a metaphorical heavyweight. Of these definitions, the first is the oldest (mid- to early 1800s). Whether sports or some other activity brought this meaning about is hard to say. But the other forms of scoring—sexual or otherwise—are twentieth-century constructs. As a result, they likely came from sports, which had defined what it meant to score for most mainstream people by that point.

Start from scratch: To make something from the beginning, usually with nothing preprepared, such as in cooking; also *up to scratch* for meeting the required standard. The sporting origin of the *scratch line* is a matter of much discussion: Nineteenth-century boxers used scratches to mark the location where they needed to stand at the beginning of a fight and at the start of subsequent rounds. Runners and horses also had lines on the ground for early starting spots. Both the bowler and the batter in cricket create scratch lines to mark their areas. So which was first? Cricket appears to have the oldest use of the word (1778, according to the *Oxford English Dictionary*). But all of them have meanings—an opening point for worthy competitors—that work well with the eventual idioms.

Step up one's game: To elevate one's performance. While *upping your game* may have come earlier, *stepping it up* could be found in newspapers beginning in the 1930s. In that decade, references from both tennis and golf existed. For example, in 1939, an Associated Press article wondered whether tennis great Don Budge would be able to "step up his game to the peak necessary to whip [Ellsworth] Vines." Three years earlier, an article on golf guides written by pro links player Chester Horton said the books would "help you step up your game."

That's the way the ball bounces: Describes lack of control over outcomes. Before late nineteenth-century mass production homogenized every sphere and orb with which we play, each ball was unique. Athletes had to navigate a ball's imperfections as much as they had to understand the opposing team. Even with factory-made balls, external circumstances like the field and player performance can keep even the most astute fan guessing. Such uncertainty led to the phrase's development in the 1950s. By the end of the decade, it was so frequently used in a nonsporting context that it was already considered by many to be cliché.

ENDNOTES

Introduction

"My hat is in the ring," Gabriel Snyder, "February 29: Theodore Roosevelt Says Yes!; Paparazzi at Harvard," *The Wire*, February 29, 2012 • "You hit . . . a home run," Scott Horsley, "In Diplomacy, Obama Aims To 'Hit Singles,' Not Swing For Fences," NPR.org, April 29, 2014 • "relate closely . . . people," William Safire, *Safire's Political Dictionary* (New York: Oxford University Press, 2008), 695 • "language meant . . . unconsciously," Francine Hardaway, "Foul Play: Sports Metaphors as Public Doublespeak," *College English* (September 1976, Vol. 31, No. 1), 78–79 • "to make lies . . . respectable," Geoffrey Nunberg, "Simpler Terms; If It's 'Orwellian,' It's Probably Not," *New York Times*, June 22, 2003 • "Son, I think . . . struck out," *The Onion*, "I Wish I Could Get Through To You With a Sports Analogy, Young Man," April 8, 2014.

Chapter 1: BASEBALL

"I'd say . . . renovation," Charles McGrath, "Law & Order & Law & Order & Law & Order & Law and Order . . ." *New York Times Magazine*, September 21, 2003.

Ballpark figure: "guesstimate," *The Arizona Republic*, "U.S. vehicles in Saigon beyond guesstimate," October 11, 1968, Sec. E, p. 1 • "The ballpark . . . 'in this world'" William Safire

(N.Y. Times News Service), "Baseball: How the national pastime has affected everyday language," *Lawrence* (Kansas) *Journal-World*, June 28, 1981, 4A.

Batting a thousand: "batting a thousand . . . honors," *The Bee* (Danville, Virginia), (No headline • first column), March 14, 1927, 6 • "A home run . . . thousand percent," *New York Times*, "Ruth Appeal For Funds." May 1, 1921 (from *New York Times* digital archives).

Big leagues: "The Big Leagues," *The Bradford Era*, "The Big League," August 15, 1890, 1 • "big-league candidate," Franklin P. Adams, *New York Tribune*, August 21, 1917, 9 (as quoted in *The Dickson Baseball Dictionary, Third Edition*).

Catbird seat: "She must be . . . down South," James Thurber, *Thurber on Crime* (ed. Robert Lopresti) (New York: Mysterious Press, 1991), 2 • "poetry's catbird seat," *The Biloxi Sun Herald* (Mississippi), "Gulfport native Trethewey appointed US poet laureate," June 7, 2012, 2.

Curveball: "Go stand . . . optical illusion," Whitney Shoemaker, "Scientist Proves Baseball Does Curve," *Milwaukee Sentinel*, March 29, 1959, 2-C.

Different ball game: "Whole New Ball Game," advertisement, "At Copper

City It's A Whole New Ball Game," *The Montana Standard* (Butte, Montana), October 24, 1974, 22.

Get your turn at bat: "All that . . . accorded the individual," Helen Granat, *Wisdom Through the Ages, Book Two* (Victoria, Canada: Trafford Publishing, 2006), 150 • "turn at bat," Ja'Net Dubois and Oren Waters, *Movin' on Up (Theme to the Jeffersons)*, released 1975 • "in regular turn," Peter Morris, *A Game of Inches* (Chicago: Ivan R. Dee, 2006), 21.

Grandstanding: "The appeal . . . the process," J.J. Dickinson, "Battle for Control of Next Congress," *The Washington Post*, August 19, 1906, 2.

Jazz: "pep . . . vigor," Ben Zimmer, "'Jazz': A Tale of Three Cities," *Visual Thesaurus* (www.visualthesarus.com), June 8, 2009 • "Blues Is Jazz . . . Blues," Dave Wilton, "jazz," Wordorigins.org, June 26, 2007.

On the fly: "That has mainly . . . the moment," and "attracted to . . . expressiveness," Ed Folsom, *Walt Whitman's Native Representations* (Cambridge, UK: Cambridge University Press, 1997), 50.

Out in left field: "that was . . . left field," Arnold Shaw, "The Vocabulary of Tin-Pan Alley Explained," *Notes* (Second Series, December 1949, Vol. 7, No. 1), 48.

Pinch-hit: "pinch," *The Fort Wayne* (Indiana) *Sentinel*, "Let Well Enough Alone," May 15, 1900, 12 • "an instance . . . special difficulty," *Oxford English Dictionary* (*pinch* entry), www.OED.com.

Rain check: "If you expect . . . rain checks," *Oxford English Dictionary* (*rain check* entry), www.OED.com.

Right off the bat: "The Devil . . . muscle men," George P. Upton, *Letters of Peregrin Pickle* (Chicago: The Western News Co., 1869), 38 • "began business . . . would say," *New Albany* (Indiana) *Evening Tribune*, "Solons Hard at Work," January 10, 1900, 4.

Rounding the bases: Metaphor for getting it on: "If you're . . . being rude," United Press, "Co-Eds Lament 'Date Behavior'," *The Hammond* (Indiana) *Times*, April 7, 1939, 13.

Step up to the plate: "while daring greatly," Charles Morris, *Battling for the Right: The Life-Story of Theodore Roosevelt* (Chicago: W.E. Scull, 1910), 355.

Swinging for the fences: "If I deliberately . . . I don't," Cal Ripken Jr. and Mike Bryan, *The Only Way I Know* (New York: Viking Penguin, 1997), 194 • "If I'd tried . . . six hundred," www.baberuth.com/quotes.

Switch-hitter: "a bisexual person," *Oxford English Dictionary* (*switch-hitter* entry), www.OED.com • "Greg is . . . that year," Ann Landers, "Ann Landers Answers Your Problems," *Havre* (Montana) *Daily News*, March 12, 1975, 7.

Chapter 2: BASKETBALL

"If it . . . no foul," *CBS News Transcripts*, "James Cameron, Director of 'Titanic,' Discusses Making The Most Expensive Movie Ever Made," *CBS This Morning*, December 19, 1997.

Baller: "the perceived . . .
ostentatiously," *Oxford English
Dictionary* (*baller* entry), www.OED
.com • "*NBA Ballers* . . . to get it," Pete
Metzger, "Staying In; Game Reviews;
Playoff madness at your fingertips,"
Los Angeles Times, April 15, 2004, E28.

Going one-on-one: "delighted with . . .
against," Steve Gerstel (United Press
International), "HHH and McGovern
nix Wallace as VP Candidate," *Bucks
County* (Pennsylvania) *Courier Times*,
May 31, 1972, 10.

Go-to guy: "Derek . . . crucial
situations," United Press International,
"Sports News," April 4, 1985 •
"become . . . guy," Jim Thomas, "Smith
gets 41 points in Clippers' win," *Daily
Breeze* (Torrance, California), April 4,
1985, E3 • "the go-to man," William
Gildea, "Douglas: Modest Secret, Bona
Fide Talent," *The Washington Post*,
April 4, 1985, B6 • "All the better . . .
two points," Tony Kornheiser, "Bound
for the Lottery," *The Washington Post*,
December 13, 1988, E1.

Home court advantage: "home
officiating advantage," Bob Rule
(Newspaper Enterprise Association),
"It's the Officiating: 'Home Court
Advantage' is Evil of College
Basketball," *Sandusky* (Ohio) *Register*,
February 7, 1963, 26 • "is usually . . . in
basketball," Dave Park (International
News Service), "Hogs Take Early
Lead in '41 Race," *Austin* (Texas) *Daily
Texan*, January 14, 1941, 3 • "It doesn't
mean . . . ," Tom Enlund, "Home-court
advantage: Does it really matter?" *The
Milwaukee Journal*, April 29, 1984, 8.

In your face: "phrase to be . . . an
opponent," Chuck Wielgus and
Alexander Wolf, *The Back-In-Your-Face
Guide to Pick-Up Basketball* (New York:
Dodd, Mead & Co., 1986), 224–25.

No harm, no foul: "In Dr. Carlson's . . .
made greater," *The News* (Newport,
Rhode Island), "Controversial
Subject," October 21, 1954, 12.

Chapter 3: Football

"[Americans] know . . . the ball," David
Gritten, "A Director's Method Amid
the Madness," *Los Angeles Times*,
December 31, 1994, 16.

Armchair quarterback: "the
armchair . . . of hindsight," *Salt Lake
City Tribune*, "Police Probe Clears
Rookie of Improper Gun Use,"
September 30, 1971, B1.

Blind side: "the unguarded . . . or
thing," *Oxford English Dictionary*
(*blind side* entry), www.OED.com. •
"It was called . . . heads off," Michael
Lewis, *The Blind Side* (Movie Tie-in
Edition) (New York: W.W. Norton &
Co., 2009), 21.

Call an audible: "Well . . . to
audibilize," Associated Press, "The
Play Is The Thing If Brown Calls
It," *The Press Courier* (Oxnard,
California), December 4, 1969, 8 •
"If your . . . call SI," advertisement,
"Sports Illustrated cordially invites
you to participate in our second half,"
New York Times, July 8, 1969, 88.

Cheerleader: "Here and there . . .
in Europe," Alexis de Tocqueville,
Democracy in America (New York:

J. & H.G. Langley, 1840), 142 · "one of . . . Brown game," *Oxford English Dictionary* (*cheerleader* entry), www.OED.com.

End run: "Long runs . . . success," A. Alonzo Stagg and Henry L. Williams, *A Scientific and Practical Treatise on American Football for Schools and Colleges* (New York: D. Appleton & Company, 1894), 251 · "I had . . . Americans call it," Winston Churchill, "Closing The Ring," *The Advertiser* (Adelaide, Australia), October 25, 1951, 2.

Hail Mary: "It was . . . catches it," William Wallace, "Bengals' Rally Falls Short in 31-28 Loss," *New York Times*, December 29, 1975, 21.

Huddle: "with vigor," Maynard Brichford, *Bob Zuppke: The Life and Football Legacy of the Illinois Coach* (Jefferson, NC: McFarland & Co., 2008), 27 · "gives too . . . haven't any," Billy Evans, "Billy Evans Says," *The Daily Mail* (Hagerstown, Maryland), January 21, 1927, 11 · "a mass . . . confusion" and "a confused crowd," *Oxford English Dictionary* (*huddle* entry), www.OED.com.

Ivy League: "our eastern ivy colleges," *Penn Current* (Philadelphia), "Ask Benny: The Ivy League, from fiction to facts," October 17, 2002.

Monday morning quarterback: "The answer . . . quarterbacks," Associated Press, "Football Critics Chided by Wood," *New York Times*, December 5, 1931, 22.

Time-out: "Time taken . . . in progress," Walter Camp and Lorin F. Deland, *Football* (Boston: Houghton, Mifflin & Co., 1896), 61.

Chapter 4: HOCKEY

Thomas Ricks, "No Power Play, Rumsfeld Says; Pentagon Chief Defends General's Nomination to Be CIA Director," *Washington Post*, May 10, 2006, A.03..

Face-off: "faced," W. George Beers, *Lacrosse: The National Game of Canada* (Montreal: Dawson Brothers, 1869), 33.

A brief game changer: Other skating sports: "In skating . . . our speed," Ralph Waldo Emerson, *The Early Lectures of Ralph Waldo Emerson*, Volume 2 (Cambridge, Massachusetts: Harvard University Printing Office, 1964), 243.

Hat trick: "dynamic . . . 'power play,'" The Canadian Press, "Shore Is Selected For Hockey Honors," *New York Times*, April 18, 1933, 18.

Chapter 5: SOCCER

"I'm ordinary . . . on," Chrissy Iley, "Uplifting experience," *Sunday Times* (London), October 17, 2004, Style, 10.

Kick off: "I'm going . . . my shoes." *Oxford English Dictionary* (*kick off* entry), www.OED.com · "kickoff . . . by tossing," Nugent Robinson, *Collier's Cyclopedia of Social and Commercial Information* (New York: Peter Fenelon Collier, 1882), 385.

Moving the goalposts: "If we . . . students' minds," Marjorie Carpenter, "Stimulating Students to Make Critical Value Judgments," (essay in) *The Two Ends of the Log: Earning and Teaching in Today's College*, by Russell M. Cooper (Minneapolis: University of Minnesota Press, 1958), 89.

Political football: "a political . . . all parties," *The Farmers' Journal and Agricultural Advertiser*, untitled, May 22, 1826, 165.

Soccer mom: "With the . . . photograph forms," Julie Kendrick, "Helpful 'soccer moms' standouts in their field," *The Daily Herald* (Arlington Heights, Illinois), October 5, 1984, sec. 1, p. 5.

Chapter 6: AUTO RACING

Marilyn Malara, "Nick Cannon shares message from hospital bed: 'Don't worry, temporary pit stop,'" www.upi.com, July 23, 2015.

Pedal to the metal: "As they . . . the metal," Bill Gilbert, "Bill Gilbert Morning News Sports Writer," *Florence* (South Carolina) *Morning News*, October 21, 1975, 5-A.

Pit stop: "It was . . . for free," Motorsport.com, "Evolution of the pit stop—the early years," August 26, 2010.

Language legacy of the Indianapolis 500: "A qualified . . . ten-mile run," Associated Press, "Brawner Earns Gold: Don Davis Unhurt in 750-Foot Skid," *The Arizona Republic*, May 20, 1961, 37.

Chapter 7: BILLIARDS (POOL)

"I didn't . . . in there," Cal Fussman, "The Talent" *Esquire*, January 1, 2008, 96.

Behind the eight ball: "He was . . . never a nine" and "There I am . . . eight-ball blues," George Bugbee, *Memphis Press-Scimitar*; "Grayson's Scoreboard: Peterson Credits a New Yorker, Alliie Flint, With Giving Birth to 'Behind the Eight Ball,'" *The Capital Times* (Madison, Wisconsin), January 20, 1941, 12.

Dirty pool: "I played . . . in court," Herman Wouk, "The Caine Mutiny: Chapter XXXIII," *The Milwaukee Journal*, October 29, 1952, 3.

Running the table: "break . . . the table," *New Castle* (Pennsylvania) *News*, "Here and There In Sports Land," March 3, 1943, 13.

Chapter 8: BOWLING

"I'm sellin' . . . wax spins," Ice-T, "I'm Your Pusher," *Power* (album), 1988.

Chapter 9: BOXING

"Why don't . . . rounds," *Federal News Service*, "Interview of President George W. Bush in Roundtable with Foreign Print Media," Roosevelt Room (White House), January 4, 2008.

Blow-by-blow: "Unflinching foot . . . was met," Sir Walter Scott, *The Poetical Works of Sir Walter Scott* (Edinburgh: Adam and Charles Black, 1869), 457 • "announced . . . by blow," *Trenton* (New Jersey) *Times*, "Events in the Local

Field of Sport," August 27, 1900, 3 ·
"blow . . . in detail," *The Post-Standard*
(Syracuse, New York), "Unequaled
Account of To-Day's Battle," July 4,
1910, 9 · "The story . . . blow," *Sandusky*
(Ohio) *Star-Journal*, "The Story 'Blow
By Blow,'" July 3, 1919, 1.

Boxers who never do any fighting:
"on intimate . . . greats," *New
York Times*, "Jacob Golomb, 58, A
Manufacturer," August 25, 1951, 9.

Floored: "up to his . . . *floored*," Kasia
Boddy, *Boxing: A Cultural History*
(London: Reaktion Books, 2008), 56.

Glass jaw: "The whole . . . slightest
jar," *The Indianapolis Sun*, "Have
Glass Jaws," December 9, 1904, 8 ·
"a newspaper . . . used it," *Popular
Mechanics*, "Knockout Analysis Takes
It on the Chin," *Sun-Sentinel* (Fort
Lauderdale, Florida), June 26, 1988.

Heavyweight: "than walking . . . of
the world?" Thomas Hauser, *Winks
and Daggers: An Inside Look at
Another Year in Boxing* (Fayetteville,
Arkansas: University of Arkansas
Press, 2011), 136.

In your corner: "refrain . . .
expressions," Henry Downes Miles,
*Pugilistica: The History of British
Boxing*, Volume 3 (Edinburgh: John
Grant, 1906), 521 · "spaces to be . . .
bottle holders," Frank L. Dowling,
*Fights For The Championships · and
Celebrated Prize Battles* (London: Bell's
Life, 1855), 259.

On the ropes: "against the ropes,"
Pierce Egan, *Boxiana; or Sketches of
Ancient & Modern Pugilism* (London:

George Virtue, 1829), 405 · "a liquor . . .
contradiction" and "the name . . .
puppets," Francis Grose, *A Classical
Dictionary of the Vulgar Tongue*,
Second Edition (London: S. Hooper,
1788), page titled "PUZ"; "The
old . . . *victualing office*;" *The New
Monthly Magazine* Vol. II, "Jonathan
Kentucky's Journal, Vol. IV" (London:
Henry Colburn and Co., 1821), 527.

Second wind: "Smart had . . .
second wind," *The Morning Chronicle*
(London), "Boxing," November 29, 1816,
3 · "recovered second wind," *The St.
James's Chronicle and London Evening
Post*, "London," December 29, 1812, 1.

Shadow boxing: "You [s]eem . . . fight
with," Heartwell, "Continuation of
the Dialogue in Elysium begun in ours
on the 19th of November," *The General
Evening Post*, December 13, 1748, 3.

Sparring partner: "These gentlemen
. . . debate before," Thomas Jefferson
(edited by Thomas Jefferson Palmer),
*Memoirs, Correspondence and Private
Papers of Thomas Jefferson, Late
President of the United States*, Vol. 1
(London: Henry Colburn and Richard
Bentley, 1829), 9.

Take a dive: "You win . . . throw
some," Robert W. Smith, "Book World;
Greed-Ring Circus; The Black Lights:
Inside the World of Professional
Boxing," *The Washington Post*,
December 31, 1985, B3.

Throw your hat in the ring:
"Belcher . . . his antagonist," *The
Morning Chronicle* (London),
"Pugilism," November 30, 1804, 4 ·
"My hat in the ring," Gabriel Snyder,

"February 29: Theodore Roosevelt Says Yes! • Paparazzi at Harvard," *The Wire*, February 29, 2012.

Chapter 10: GOLF

"We have . . . at Lowe's," Larry the Cable Guy, "Interview with Larry the Cable Guy," Fox News Network (Hannity), February 1, 2011.

Bring your A-game: "Harbour Town . . . they say," Charles Price, "Hilton Head: Golfer's Island," *Gentlemen's Quarterly*, Summer 1969, 118 • "You'd . . . A game," Ken, Denlinger, "Crenshaw, Maltbie in Masters Lead," *The Washington Post*, April 12, 1987, C1.

Follow-through: "the club . . . is expended," *Golf: A Weekly Record of "Ye Royal and Auncient" Game*, "Advice To Young Golfers," February 13, 1891, 340.

Golf clap: "simply cup . . . five times," Randy Howe, *Golf for Weekend Warriors: A Guide to Everything from Bunkers to Birdies to Back Spasms* (Guilford, Connecticut: Lyons Press, 2005), 40.

Chapter 11: HORSE RACING

"We're . . . beheaded horse," Tim Appelo, "5 Big Trends in Tightknit Tussle," *Hollywood Reporter*, September 9, 2011, S4, 1.

By a nose: "a prodigiously . . . half a nose," *The World* (London), "Newmarket; Saturday," October 6, 1789, 3.

Caught flat-footed: "caught . . . on the play," Addie Joss, "Balls & Strikes," *San Antonio* (Texas), *Gazette*, December 28, 1907, 4.

Dark horse: "a fortunate . . . heavy betters," *St. James Chronicle and General Evening Post* (London), "Court and Fashionable News," September 17, 1822, 4 • "Lord Elgin . . . no one," *The Express* (London), "Montreal, May 14," June 1, 1847, 4.

Hands down: "The Cup . . . and Kate," Pegasus, "A Glance at Bath, and The Espom Meeting," *Bell's Life in London and Sporting Chronicle*, May 23, 1852, 4 • "It is . . . hands down," *Oxford English Dictionary* (*hands down* entry), www.OED.com.

Have a horse in the race: "If Evans . . . in the race," Frank Nye, "Iowa Political Notes," *The Cedar Rapids* (Iowa) *Gazette*, March 5, 1950, 4.

Free-for-all: "free-for-all fight," *Logansport* (Indiana) *Chronicle*, untitled, January 22, 1881, 6, and *The Daily Evening Democrat* (Shelbyville, Indiana), untitled, July 28, 1881, 4.

Home stretch: "And down . . . come!" Richard Sanidomer, " 'And Down the Stretch They Come!' (All Rights Reserved)," *New York Times*, June 5, 2015.

Horse-betting language: "Several individuals . . . their money," *Oxford English Dictionary* (*run; to also get, want, etc. a run for one's money* entry), www.OED.com • "odds-on favourite," *The Daily News* (London), "Bromley Winter Steeplechase and Hurdle

Races—Wednesday," December 13, 1877, 2.

Off to the races: "off to the races," and "boisterous . . . mirth" and "solely . . . horse-racing," *The Melbourne Argus*, "Victoria," *Australian and New Zealand Gazette*, May 22, 1869, 324 • "The day . . . be lost!" *Boston Post*, "Paris Gossip," June 1, 1865, 1.

Running mate: "Sweeping . . . his running mate," *The Fifth Reader* (Philadelphia: E.H. Butler & Co., 1883), 335 • "suffered under . . . give up," *Supplement to Bell's Life in London*, "Great Trotting Match In America For Ten Thousand Dollars!" June 12, 1859, 1 • "Progress . . . to Time." *Annual Report of the State Superintendent of Public Education Thomas W. Conway to the General Assembly of Louisiana for the year 1871* (New Orleans: The Republican Office, 1872), 148.

Shoo-in: "'shoo in' . . . 'shoo,'" *The Washington Post*, "Two Jockeys Ruled Off • Strong-arm Play at Magruder Rebuked by Judge Carter," December 20, 1896, 8 • "If I had . . . with it," *The Washington Post*, "Gossip of the Turf," December 21, 1896, 8.

Straight from the horse's mouth: "reading . . . tipping papers," *Indiana Evening Gazette*, "German Likes Sport • Goes to Races," July 14, 1920, 8 • "A troop . . . horse's mouth," Aldous Huxley, *Brave New World* (New York: RosettaBooks, 2000), 4.

Track or racecourse?: "We must trot . . . Buchanan," *Indiana State Sentinel*, "Washington Correspondence," March 4, 1842, 4.

Wild-goose chase: "Happiness . . . never attained," David J. Brewer (editor), *The World's Best Essays from the Earliest Period to The Present Time*, Vol. X (St. Louis: Ferd. P. Kaiser, 1900), 3871.

Chapter 12: TENNIS

CQ Transcriptions, "President Barack Obama Delivers Weekly Radio Address," September 5, 2015.

A brief game changer: Badminton: "To keep . . . last night," Francis Grose, *A Classical Dictionary of the Vulgar Tongue*, Second Edition (London: S. Hooper, 1788), page titled "KEN."

Unforced error: "Ah yes . . . tennis court," Billie Jean King and Greg Hoffman, *Tennis Love: A Parents' Guide to the Sport* (New York: McMillan Publishing Co, 1978), 38 • "under any . . . opponent's stroke," and "The forced . . . things out," Ben Rothenberg, "Unforced Error Is Unloved Statistic Among Players," *New York Times*, March 10, 2013, SP, 11.

Chapter 13: TRACK AND FIELD (RUNNING)

"Once in . . . of measurement," Business Desk, "Steve Jobs: 1955–2011," *Los Angeles Times*, October 6, 2011, AA9.

Hop, skip, and jump: "A hop . . . of indicting," John Wolcot, *The Works of Peter Pindar* (London: John Walker, 1797), 48 • "never can . . . to letter," *The Monthly Mirror*, "Review of Literature," November 1, 1797, 281.

Jump the gun: "Half a dozen . . . not do it," Malcolm W. Ford, "Sprinters," *Outing*, May 1891, 87.

A brief game changer: Unsportsmanlike language: "Ellen Bond . . . somebody says," *Oxford English Dictionary* (*rebound* entry), www.OED .com • "the Bigfoot . . . origins," Jennifer Schuessler, "The Whole Nine Yards About a Phrase's Origin," *New York Times*, December 26, 2012.

Chapter 14: WRESTLING

Andy Greene, "Joan Rivers: The Lost Rolling Stone Interview," September 4, 2014, www.rollingstone.com/tv/ features/joan-rivers-the-lost-rolling- stone-interview-20140904.

Go to the mat: "Burns . . . Hale 147," *The* (Indianapolis) *Sun*, "Burns and Hale to Meet," January 29, 1897, 8.

No holds barred: "no holds . . . throttling," *The Galveston* (Texas) *Daily News*, "Sporting Topics, Wresting Match at Chicago," June 21, 1898, 6.

Say (or cry) uncle: "act of . . . mercy," worldwidewords.org, "Say (or cry) Uncle," www.worldwidewords.org/ qa/qa-say1.htm.

Stranglehold: "Don't murder . . . spectators," *The Daily Record* (Lawrence, Kansas), "Strangled By a Wrestler," February 27, 1892, 1 • "very properly . . . wrestling code," George Kachenschmidt, *Complete Science of Wrestling* (O'Faolain Patriot, 2012 • originally published 1909), 143 (e-book).

FREE AGENTS

Head in the game: "Jake always . . . this trade," *Buffalo Center* (Iowa) *Tribune*, "Buy your school shoes of Mallory Hofius," August 19, 1897, 5.

Keeping your eye on the ball: "kept his eye . . . a considerable distance," W. H. G. Kingston, *Schoolboy Days • or, Ernest Bracebridge* (Boston: Ticknor & Fields, 1869), 74 • "all you . . . the ball," *The Brooklyn Eagle*, "Wit and Humor," *Liberty* (Indiana) *Weekly Herald*, November 29, 1865, 4 • "Keep your eye . . . you pay for," advertisement, "Keep your eye on the ball," *The Washington Post*, June 25, 1917, 5.

Oddball: "Oddball," Larry Dale, "Sports Roundup," *Blytheville* (Arkansas) *Courier News*, November 15, 1945, 6.

Playing catch-up: "forced . . . catch up," *The Decatur Review* (Illinois), "Elkhart Gives Scare, But Decatur High Wins 19 to 11," January 6, 1930, 17 • "the allies . . . the time," John Gould, "Furthermore and However," *Wichita* (Texas) *Daily Times*, June 3, 1940, 4.

Race against time: "Ass race against time." *The Sporting Magazine*, "Ass Race against Time," July 1809, 195.

Step up one's game: "step up . . . Vines," Dillon Graham (Associated Press), "Vinnie Richards, First Pro Tennis Star, Likes Vines Over Budge," *Arizona Republic*, January 3, 1939, 4 (section two) • "help you . . . game," Chester Horton, "Good Golf," *San Antonio Press*, August 7, 1936, 11.

FURTHER READING

So that you wouldn't have to, I delved into scores of books and a vast variety of other sources on language, sports, and sports language for this volume. But if you're looking for some additional materials generally on etymology or specifically on words and phrases from the world of athletes, here are some options.

Ammer, Christine. *Southpaws & Sunday Punches and Other Sporting Expressions.* New York: Dutton Adult, 1993.

Barnhart, Robert K. *The Barnhart Concise Dictionary of Etymology: The Origins of American English Words.* New York: HarperCollins, 1995.

Considine, Tim. *The Language of Sport.* London: Routledge, 1998.

Dalzell, Tom, and Terry Victor, eds. *The New Partridge Dictionary of Slang and Unconventional English*, 2nd ed. London: Routledge, 2013.

Dickson, Paul. *The Dickson Baseball Dictionary*, 3rd ed. New York: W.W. Norton & Co, 2009.

Flavell, Linda, and Roger Flavell. *Dictionary of Idioms and Their Origins.* London: Kyle Cathie, 1992.

Grose, Francis. *A Classical Dictionary of the Vulgar Tongue.* London: S. Hooper, 1788.

Hendrickson, Robert. *The Facts on File Encyclopedia of Words and Phrase Origins,* 4th ed. New York: Checkmark Books, 2008.

Oxford English Dictionary (www.oed.com).

Palmatier, Robert A., and Harold L. Ray. *Dictionary of Sports Idioms.* Chicago: National Textbook Company, 1993.

Partridge, Eric. *Origins: A Short Etymological Dictionary of Modern English,* 4th ed. London: Routledge, 1966.

Partridge, Eric. Revised and updated edition edited by Paul Beale. *A Dictionary of Catchphrases, American and British, from the Sixteenth Century to the Present Day.* Lanham, Maryland: Scarborough House, 1992.

Safire, William. *Safire's Political Dictionary.* New York: Oxford University Press, 2008.

ACKNOWLEDGMENTS

Gratitude for anything I do (whether it's writing books or other endeavors) always begins with my wife, Jennifer, and my two children, Miller and Becca. Your love, humor, patience, and support sustain me.

As for the nuts and bolts of this book, a huge thanks goes to Dan Snierson, Lionel Chetwynd, and Michael Chetwynd. Each of you were incredibly kind to put aside time to read drafts of this volume and help me sharpen this work. My editor at Ten Speed Press, Lisa Westmoreland, also deserves full-throated praise for her considerable contributions to this project.

I reached out to numerous friends along the way for advice and assistance on various aspects of this book, and I'd be remiss if I didn't give them shout-outs. Thanks goes to Keith Blackmore, David Block, Zak Brown, Melissa Chesman, Tom Dart, Thom Geier, Jonny Gould, Erik Janssen, Billy Koch, Alen and Heidi Lang, Tracy Ma, Brian Regan, Clive Russell, Joe Sawinski, Lenny Shulman, John Simons, Lynne Snierson, Erin Sorce, Paul Swydan, John Thorn, Andrew Wolfberg, and Tim Zimmermann. In addition, a special note of appreciation goes to Gary Cohen. Without his essential logistical assistance, I would have struggled to put together much of my research.

This book is basically about etymology, which is the study of word origins and histories. Through my efforts, I learned firsthand that this discipline is more about creative detective work than straightforward scientific evaluation. To put it another way, there is rarely a smoking gun that proves the beginnings of a word or phrase. To that end, I'm indebted to all the word sleuths who have come before me and offered theories and clues. First and foremost, there are the editors and contributors to the *Oxford English Dictionary*. That considerable work served as a priceless first point of reference.

Beyond that, there are too many others to fully name, but they include Christine Ammer, Robert K. Barnhart, Paul Dickson, Robert Hendrickson, Robert Palmatier, Eric Partridge, Harold L. Ray, William Safire, and Ben Zimmer. Also, I send words of praise to the folks who run such useful word-origin websites as the Phrase Finder (www.phrases.org.uk), the Word Detective (www.word-detective.com), and World Wide Words (www.worldwidewords.org).

ABOUT THE AUTHOR

 Josh Chetwynd is a journalist, broadcaster, and author. He has served as a staff reporter for *USA Today*, the *Hollywood Reporter*, and *U.S. News & World Report*, and his writing has also appeared in such publications as the *Wall Street Journal*, the *Times* (of London), the *Harvard Negotiation Law Review*, and *Variety*. As a broadcaster, he has worked for BBC Radio, among other outlets. In terms of his sports bona fides, he primarily earned them on the baseball diamond, where he played at the NCAA Division I college level for Northwestern University and had professional stints in both the United States for the Zanesville Greys in the independent Frontier League and abroad for Sweden's Oskarshamn BK in Europe. This is his sixth book, having previously written on sports three times. His 2011 effort, *The Secret History of Balls: The Stories Behind the Things We Love to Catch, Whack, Throw, Kick, Bounce, and Bat*, was named an NPR best book that year. He lives in Denver, Colorado, with his wife and two children. Visit www.JoshChetwynd.com.

INDEX OF IDIOMS AND WORDS

The following is an alphabetical list of all the phrases and terms covered and where you can find them in this book. The italicized items are those that don't have full entries but are mentioned in the text. Note that this list contains expressions/words that don't have sports origins but come up in this volume because people sometimes assume they began in the athletic world.

Above par, 135
Air ball, 52
All bets are off, 188
All-star, 176
Also-ran, 138
Armchair quarterback, 56

Back of the net, 85
Backing a horse, 147
Backing the wrong horse, 147
Bad break, 98
Bad call, 188
Ball is at one's feet, 166
Ball is in your court, 164
Baller, 44
Ballpark figure, 8
Bandy, 74
Batting a thousand, 9
Beating somebody to the punch, 121
Behind the eight ball, 96

Below par, 135
Below the belt, 108
Benched, 189
Bending over backwards, 187
Bias, 104
Big leagues, the, 10
Big-leaguing, 11
Blindsided, 56
Blitz, 176
Blow-by-blow, 109
Bonk, 170
Bowled over, 189
Boxer shorts (Boxers), 114
Boxing Day, 176
Boxing tonsils, 80
Bring your A-game, 130
Bruiser, 111
Bursting your bubble, 93
Bush leaguer, 11
Bush leagues, 11
By a nose, 138

Calling an audible, 57
Carry the ball, 71
Catbird seat, 16
Catch as catch can, 182
Caught flat-footed, 139
Caught off base, 25
Cheapskate, 77
Cheerleader, 58
Clear a hurdle, 189
Coach (coaching), 60
Counterpunch, 121
Cover all the bases, 12
Covering your bases, 12
Curveball, 13

Dark horse, 141
Dead center, 140
Dead heat, 140
Dead ringer, 140
Different ball game, 16
Dirty pool, 97
Doing somersaults, 187
Don't count me out, 111
Don't look a gift horse in the mouth, 160

Don't pull any punches, 121
Down and out, 110
Down for the count, 110
Down to the wire, 161
Dropped the ball, 190

Early doors, 85
End run, 59

Face-off, 78
Fair play, 190
Fan, 18
Fast track, 148
Final stretch, 150
Finish line, 190
Finishing out of the money, 138
Firing on all cylinders, 90
First out of the gate, 142
Flake (flaky), 20
Flat out, 90
Floored, 111
Fluke, 101
Follow-through, 131
Free-for-all, 152
Front-runner, 190
Full-court press, 45
Fumble, 64

Game changer, 191
Game face, 191
Game over, 191
Game plan, 61
Game-time decision, 191
Gentlemen, start your engines, 92

Get your turn at bat, 19
Getting to first base, 34
Glass jaw, 112
Go a couple of rounds, 113
Go a few rounds, 113
Go the distance, 192
Go to the mat, 180
Go to your corners, 117
Going one-on-one, 46
Going to bat for [someone], 31
Golf clap, 131
Good break, 99
Good call, 188
Go-to guy, 82
Grandstand quarterbacks, 86
Grandstanding, 21
Ground game, 62
Ground rules, 192
Grudge match, 192

Had a good innings, 14
Hail Mary, 63
Handoff, 64
Hands down, 146
Hat trick, 76
Have a ball, 176
Have a horse in the race, 146
Have the ball at one's foot, 85
Head fake, 192
Head in the game, 193
Head start, 193
Head over heels, 187

Head-the-ball, a, 85
Heavyweight, 114
Hit, a, 14
Hit and run, 22
Hit the wall, 170
Hitting a guy when he's down, 108
Hitting one out of the ballpark, 22
Hockey moms, 86
Home court advantage, 47
Home field advantage, 47
Home run, 22
Home stretch, 150
Hop, skip, and jump, 170
Horses for courses, 148
Huddle, 64

In the ballpark, 8
In the fast lane, 90
In the running, 147
In the tank, 126
In your corner, 116
In your face, 48
Inside baseball, 23
Inside edge, the, 76
Inside track, 148
Ivy League, 69

Jazz, 26
Jump the gun, 171

Keep it up, 164
Keep the ball rolling, 177
Keep your eye on the ball, 194

Keeping score, 193

Kick off, 82

Kingpin, 105

Knocked down, 117

Knocking the daylights out of someone, 111

Knockout, 117

Knowing all the angles, 196

Knowing the score, 193

Leading with your chin, 112

Level playing field, 194

Lightweight, 115

Low blow, 108

Lucky break, 98

Make a play, 194

Mano a mano, 154

Marathon, 173

Miscue, 99

Moment of truth, the, 158

Monday morning quarterback, 67

Moving the goalposts, 82

Mulligan, 132

My bad, 49

NASCAR dads, 86

Neck and neck, 150

No harm, no foul, 80

No holds barred, 180

Oddball, 195

Odds-on favorite, 145

Off and running, 154

Off base, 24

Off his base, 25

Off to a flying start, 154

Off to the races, 151

Old head in the game, 193

On the bench, 189

On the bubble, 92

On the fly, 28

On the rebound, 177

On the right (or wrong) track, 149

On the ropes, 118

On the sideline(s), 195

On track, 149

On your game, 195

One-two punch, 121

Out for the count, 111

Out in left field, 29

Out of left field, 30

Out of the running, 147

Out of your (or my) league, 12

Own goal, 85

Pack a punch, 120

Par for the course, 134

Pass the baton, 174

Pedal to the metal, 90

Pee like a racehorse, 154

Photo finish, 155

Pinch-hit, 30

Pinning down, 182

Pit stop, 91

Play ball, 32

Play hardball, 32

Playbook, 62

Playing catch-up, 196

Playing the angles, 196

Playing the field, 145

Pole position, 92

Political football, 84

Power play, 79

Pulling punches, 121

Punch line, 121

Punch-drunk, 121

Punching above your weight, 121

Punching bag, 121

Punt, 68

Quarterback, 60

Quick off the mark, 178

Quick (or slow) out of the blocks, 175

Race against the clock, 196

Race against time, 196

Rain check, 33

Raise (or lower) the bar, 178

Right off the bat, 33

Ringside seats, 119

Roll with the punches, 121

Rookie, 176

Root, to (or rooting), 36

Rope-a-dope, 118

Rough and tumble, 181
Route one, 85
Run for your money, a, 144
Run interference, 216
Run its course, 197
Run out the clock, 197
Run with the ball, 71
Runner-up, 198
Running circles around someone, 76
Running mate, 156
Running the table, 100
Runoff, 197
Run-up, the, 198

Saved by the bell, 122
Say (or cry) uncle, 182
Score, to, 198
Screwball, 15
Second wind, 123
Seeing red, 159
Set the bar high (or low), 178
Shadow boxing, 124
Shoo-in, 157
Skate, to, 77
Skating circles, 76
Skating on thin ice, 77
Slam dunk, 51
Soccer mom, 86
Softball question, 38
Spar, to, 126
Sparring partner, 125
Spitballing, 40

Springboard, 187
Square off, 122
Start from scratch, 198
Starting line, 190
Step up one's game, 199
Step up to the plate, 36
Sticky wicket, a, 15
Straight from the horse's mouth, 160
Stranglehold, 185
Strike out, 38
Stud, 142
Stymie, 134
Suits you to a tee, 136
Sunday punch, 121
Swinging for the fences, 39
Swinging from your heels, 41
Switch-hitter, 42

Take a dive, 126
Take all comers, 128
Take it on the chin, 112
Take the full count, 111
Take the long count, 111
Taking a page out of another's playbook, 62
Taking one for the team, 32
Taking the bull by the horns, 159
Tanking, 126
Tee up, 135
Teed off, 136

That's a red card, 85
That's the way the ball bounces, 199
The (nuclear) football, 65
There's the rub, 106
This isn't my first rodeo, 159
Throw in the towel, 127
Throw up a brick, 51
Throw your hat in the ring, 128
Throwing in the sponge, 127
Ticky tack, 52
Time-out, 71
Tonsil hockey, 80
Too close to call, 147
Touch base, 12
Track record, 149
Trifecta, 145

Under the wire, 161
Unforced error, 166
Up to par, 135
Up to scratch, 198
Upping your game, 199

Where the rubber meets the road, 90
Whole new ball game, 18
Wild-goose chase, 162
Wire to wire, 161
Wrestling, 186